ENTREPRENEURSHIP IN PACIFIC ASIA

PAST, PRESENT & FUTURE

ENTREPRENEURSHIP IN PACIFIC ASIA

PAST, PRESENT & FUTURE

LEO PAUL DANA

BA, MBA, PhD

Senior Advisor
World Association for Small & Medium Enterprises
&
Deputy Director
MBA (International Business) Programme
Nanyang Technological University
&
Associate Director
ENDEC Entrepreneurship Development Centre

Singapore

With a foreword by Professor Jerome A. Katz, PhD,
Senior Vice President for Research & Publications,
International Council for Small Business, St. Louis, USA.

World Scientific
Singapore • New Jersey • London • Hong Kong

Published by

World Scientific Publishing Co. Pte. Ltd.

P O Box 128, Farrer Road, Singapore 912805

USA office: Suite 1B, 1060 Main Street, River Edge, NJ 07661

UK office: 57 Shelton Street, Covent Garden, London WC2H 9HE

British Library Cataloguing-in-Publication Data
A catalogue record for this book is available from the British Library.

ISBN 981-02-3929-7
ISBN 981-02-3930-0 (pbk)

Printed in Singapore.

Dedicated to Ima, Perto and Teresa

Foreword

On the eve of the Western calendar's millennium, journalists and legislators already describe the future as the "century of the entrepreneur." The potential, continuing growth of economies world-wide, spurred by the growth of entrepreneurship, represents an economic and social marvel of tremendous importance to us all; but if the impact of entrepreneurship in the future is seen as important and undeniable, the cultural form that entrepreneurship takes is much less clear.

In the 6th and 7th centuries, the dominant entrepreneurial culture was that of the Phoenicians. In the 10th and 11th centuries it was the great caravan drivers of Persia and China. In the 14th and 15th centuries, the adventurers of Spain and Portugal. In the 17th and 18th, the English, and arguably, in the 19th and 20th, it was the inventors of the United States. Carnegie, DuPont, Edison, Ford, Disney, Rouse, Gates, and Jobs – these were the names of individuals whose inventions changed the way that the world worked and played. The culture of entrepreneurship they fostered reflected their culture surely and clearly. Can we believe that theirs will be the first entrepreneurial culture to truly endure, dwarfing the emergence of other cultures to future dominance?

What makes an entrepreneurial culture dominant? It is partly hard work, fuelled by energy, technologies and other ideas, partly geography (what Americans call "being in the right place at the right time") and to be honest, partly luck. America, safe between two wide oceans, survived 200-plus years without a foreign attack on its mainland. It had room to grow, resources to exploit, and no natural or national enemies to threaten its people. This combination was luck. That the Americans made such powerful and profitable use of it was their good fortune.

Could other entrepreneurial cultures arise as dominant? History assures us that the answer is yes. The great search for all of us interested in entrepreneurship is to find where the next dominant entrepreneurial culture will be. And if anyone is likely to find those future stars first, it is Leo Paul Dana.

Professor Dana is considered one of the world's top experts on entrepreneurship in diverse cultures. He comes by this knowledge through personal exploration and personal experience. He has visited and worked in more nations than any other ten entrepreneurship professors. And his experience, as you will see in this volume, is not confined to the cities. He explores opportunities and entrepreneurs throughout a country, finding resources, ideas, and futures in the village, along the road, and at the market. He has seen the business world as few professors of this century have, from tin-sided factories in the grasslands, to corporate suites in megalopolises. He knows the big picture and he knows the details that form it.

In this book *Entrepreneurship in Pacific Asia: Past, Present and Future*, Dr. Dana offers his experience of the entrepreneurial cultures of this vibrant and changing region. The volume reflects his belief that here in Pacific Asia lies one of the greatest potentials for a dominant future entrepreneurial culture. In the pages that follow, he describes these nations and their forms of entrepreneurship in ways useful to the deal-maker and the legislator. He shows the overall trend and its component parts.

As always, his work is meticulous, his energy apparent, his message clear, and his style readable. What he says may not always agree with your own experiences, or interpretations, but I think you will find that his ideas will stimulate your own thinking and rethinking, and offer you insights about the people, institutions, opportunities and ideas of this dynamic region.

The stories of entrepreneurial drive and energy described in the following pages may be seen as a "shot across the bow" for some. For legislators in the region, as an incentive to let the market forces work. For legislators elsewhere, as a warning of looming competitors. For entrepreneurs everywhere, both of the above, as well as the opportunity for new sales and new alliances. It is a region full of promise, on the brink of potential greatness. To see one powerful vision of this, read on.

Jerome A. Katz, PhD
Mary Louise Murray Endowed Professor of Management
Saint Louis University
&
Senior Vice President for Research & Publications
International Council for Small Business (ICSB)

Contents

Preface

My fascination with Asia began at Expo 67 – the 1967 World's Fair, in Montreal, Canada – where I would spend hours exploring the pavilions of Asian nations.

I remember reading four years later, in *National Geographic*, that thousands of lives were sacrificed – along with billions of dollars – trying to protect Asia from communism:

> Yet our effort may ultimately fall short of success. Why? For one thing, we have neglected our homework. *We do not really know these myriad people.* We do not know whence they came; we are baffled by their thought processes (Grosvenor, 1971, p.295).

I subsequently made it my goal to learn about the lands and the peoples of Asia, their histories and policies.

The idea to put together this book was given to me in Copenhagen. It was November 1996 and I was presenting an invited faculty seminar at the Asia Research Centre of the Institute of International Economics and Management, at the Copenhagen Business School.

During my discourse, I explained that in the past, international business and the small enterprise sector were almost mutually exclusive. Internationalisation was generally limited to large corporations, while owner-managers and small-scale entrepreneurs tended to be local. In time, relaxation of government regulations opened up unprecedented opportunities, challenges, and threats to entrepreneurs and their firms. Internationalisation became an option for many; for some, it became a necessity.

Entrepreneurs in small domestic markets may find it necessary to expand internationally in order to benefit from scale economies. In vertically integrated industries, internationalisation is often a necessity for survival.

The availability of venture capital and various government programmes have facilitated the process of creating a new venture, but staying in business has become a greater challenge than it ever was before.

How should an entrepreneur – with limited time and resources – select a new location for business? Success at home does not necessarily mean success abroad. Before expanding into new territories, entrepreneurs should know about the conditions for entrepreneurship in different environments. Building a factory in a hostile environment can be an expensive mistake, while ignoring a profitable opportunity also has its costs.

Even with its economic downturn, much activity takes place in Asia. This vast continent accounts for almost half the annual growth in world. Yet, there are important differences *within* this economic zone. While Hong Kong is still influenced by laissez-faire economics, Vietnam presents opportunities within regulatory constraints. Laos has important cultural particularities and infrastructural problems.

Given that researching conditions for entrepreneurship in different countries can be challenging, many entrepreneurs cannot conduct their own research. They do not have the time and resources for comparative studies.

Since it is too time-consuming to identify the optimal course of action, entrepreneurs simply content themselves with merely acceptable options. How wonderful it would be to have easy access to information about entrepreneurship – in different environments – all in one volume! Yet, no such book existed.

Therefore, I embarked on the mission to compile information on entrepreneurship across the eastern shores of Asia, *i.e.* Pacific Asia. Here it is!

Leo-Paul Dana, BA, MBA, PhD
Deputy Director
International Business MBA Programme
Nanyang Business School
&
Associate Director
ENDEC Entrepreneurship Development Centre
Singapore

Acknowledgements

First of all, I would like to thank Teresa, for her help and encouragement during many long days and nights of research, on Saturday nights, Sundays and public holidays.

Assistance was also received from experts, from prominent institutions, around the world:

Australia (Gus Geursen, Senior Research Fellow with the Dean's Research Group at Monash University);

Canada (Richard W. Wright, Professor and Chair of International Business, at the Faculty of Management of McGill University);

England (Glenn Hook, Professor of Japanese Studies, at the Centre for Japanese Studies at the University of Sheffield, and Michael J. G. Parnwell, Professor of South-East Asian Studies at the University of Hull);

France (Evelyne Dourille-Feer, Economist at CEPII, in Paris);

Indonesia (Ridwan Gunawan, Senior Vice President of PT Astra International, in Jakarta, and Professor Tulus Tambunan of the Institute for Economic Studies, Research and Development);

Japan (Masaaki Hirano, of the Waseda University Business School in Tokyo, Professor Kenji Matsuoka of the Faculty of Economics at the Osaka University of Economics, Yoshio Sakuma, Professor at the Institute for International Economic Studies, in Tokyo, David Willis, Professor of Cultural Studies and Anthropology, at Soai University in Osaka, and Takayuki Ito of the Good Samaritan Club);

Korea (Professor Joon-Mo Yang, of the Department of Economics at Pusan National University);

New Zealand (Dr. Sarah Turner of the Department of Geography at the University of Otago, in Dunedin);

The Philippines (Salvador I. Sibayan, Luisa Solarte-Lee and Myrna R. Co, University Extension Specialists, at the Open University of the Philippines);

Singapore (Dr. Taihoon Cha, David Leong Choon Chiang, Dennis Ong Chin Siew and Dr. Jean Kwon Wook, at the Nanyang Business School of Nanyang Technological University, and Dr. Henry Wai-Chung Yeung of the Department of Geography at the National University of Singapore); and

The United States (Sophar Ear at the World Bank, Earl Honeycutt Jr., Professor of Marketing and Chair of the Department of Business Administration at Old Dominion University, in Norfolk, Virginia, Dr. David. P. Paul III, Co-Director at Monmouth University in West Long Branch, New Jersey, and Dr. Herbert Scharf of Woodmere, Long Island).

In addition I deem it appropriate to acknowledge the influence which Confucius has had on me.

> *If one learns from others, but does not think,*
> *one will be bewildered.*
> *If one thinks, but does not learn, one will peril.*

– Confucius (551-479 BC)

Chapter 1

Introduction

In this book, the word "entrepreneurship" refers to the economic undertaking of entrepreneurs. This is based on the classical definition of the word, which can be traced to the German *unternehmung* (literally: undertaking) and to the French *entreprendre* (literally: between taking). The agents of entrepreneurship are entrepreneurs (from the French *entrepreneurs,* literally: between takers). The flagships of entrepreneurship are small and medium enterprises (SMEs).

While large corporations can greatly increase their efficiency and profitability, by outsourcing to specialised enterprises of lesser scale, entrepreneurs can benefit by focusing on niche markets. When having an economy of scale is not an issue, small firms may even have comparative advantages (vis-à-vis larger ones) in assembly, mixing or finishing. Yet, entrepreneurs need not compete with large firms. Instead, large and small firms can form symbiotic relationships, offering complementary services, thus improving a society's bearing capacity. Entrepreneurship can also contribute to social development by providing local employment with relatively low levels of investment. Furthermore, the flexibility of entrepreneurs, in the absence of excessive bureaucracy, helps them respond quickly to changing needs.

Today, it is widely accepted that entrepreneurship contributes to development, with a positive effect on society, creating employment, economic expansion, a larger tax base, and more consumer well being. This is increasingly supported by research, and governments around the world have acknowledged this. Relevant literature exists about entrepreneurship in Albania (Dana, 1996a), Angola (Gray and Allison, 1997), Argentina (Dana, 1997a), Australia (Carstairs and Welch, 1982; Cavusgil, 1994; Dana, 1987a; Holmes, 1988; and Meredith, 1984), Austria (Dana, 1992a), Bangladesh (Nehrt, 1987; and Sarder, Ghosh, and Rosa, 1997), Brazil (Quesada and Mello, 1987), Brunei (Wimalatissa, 1996), Burkina Faso (Camilleri, 1997),

1

Canada (Dana, 1990c; 1993a; 1996c), the Caribbean (Dana, 1995c), China (Chau, 1995; Dana, 1999a; Dandridge and Flynn,1988; Fan, Chen and Kirby, 1996; Siu, 1995; and Williams and Li), Croatia (Martin and Grbac, 1998), Cuba (Dana, 1996e), the Czech and Slovak Republic (Rondinelli, 1991), the Czech Republic (Sacks, 1993), Egypt (Brockhaus, 1991), Estonia (Liuhto, 1996), Fiji (Meredith, 1989), France (Pache, 1996), the Former Yugoslav Republic of Macedonia (Dana, 1998b), Germany (Dana, 1994c; and Simon, 1992;1996), Ghana (Dana, 1992b), Great Britain (Gibb, 1986-7; and Ward, 1987), Greece (Dana, 1999b); Guyana (Raghunanda, 1995), Honduras (Befus, Mecon, Mescon, and Vozikis, 1988), Hungary (Hisrich and Fulop, 1995; Hisrich and Vecsenyi, 1990; Noar, 1985; and Webster, 1993), India (Gadgil, 1959; Hazlehurst 1966; and Patel, 1987), Indonesia (Geertz 1963; and Tambunan, 1992), Ireland (Walsh and Anderson, 1995), Japan (Dana, 1998a; and Morita and Oliga, 1991), Kazakhstan (Dana, 1997b), Kenya (Dana, 1993c), Laos (Dana, 1995d), Lesotho (Dana, 1997e), Malaysia (Dana, 1987b), Mexico (Grabinsky, 1996; and Silva-Castan, Prott and Anjola-Rojas, 1997), Moldova (Dana, 1997c), Mozambique (Dana, 1996d), Namibia (Dana, 1993b), the Netherlands (Bijmolt and Zwart, 1994; and Boissevain and Grotenbreg, 1987), New Zealand (Ghosh and Taylor, 1995), Nigeria (Anyansi-Archibong, 1987), Northern Ireland (Hisrich, 1988; and Jenkins, 1984), Norway (Weaver, Berkowitz and Davies, 1998), Panama (Dana, 1995a), Papua-New Guinea (Ojuka-Onedo, 1996), Peru (Dana, 1988), the Philippines (Chen, 1997), Poland (Arendarski, Mroczkowski and Sood, 1994; and Zapalska, 1997), Russia (Bruton, 1998; and Hisrich and Gratchev, 1993), Scotland (Kinsey, 1987), St. Martin (Dana, 1990a), Singapore (Dana, 1987b), Slovakia (Ivy, 1996), South Korea (Dana, 1990b; and Lee, 1998), Spain (Dana, 1995b), Swaziland (Dana, 1993d); Sweden (Holmquist and Sundin, 1988; and Johannison, 1987), Taiwan (Dana, 1994-5; and Lin, 1998), Tanzania (Van der Land and Uliwa, 1997), Togo (Dana, 1992b), the Ukraine (Ahmed, Dana, Anwar and Biedyuk, 1998), Uruguay (Dana, 1997a), Venezuela (Dana, 1996b), Vietnam (Dana, 1994a), Yugoslavia (Dana 1994d), Zimbabwe (Neshamba, 1997) and elsewhere (Dana 1994b).

Although interest in entrepreneurship as an academic discipline has spanned the globe, the phenomenon itself is expressed differently around the world. Furthermore, each government's policies affect entrepreneurship in different ways.

This book is the first of its kind, in that it assembles reports of recent research about entrepreneurship across Asia's Pacific rim. Its purpose is to give the reader a feel for the unique historical experiences and public policies affecting entrepreneurship in the Asian countries neighbouring the Pacific Ocean.

As will be shown, entrepreneurship differs greatly across this region. Cultural values, government policy and a variety of other factors, including a nation's colonial experience, affect entrepreneurship. Even the definition of "small business" varies.   In Japan, for example, the law considers an industrialist with up to 300 full-time employees to be an entrepreneur who owns a small or medium enterprise. Japanese retailers with up to 50 full-time employees and wholesalers with up to 100 full-time employees are likewise considered small-scale entrepreneurs. In Indonesia, in contrast, the government defines small industries as units of production with 5 to 20 workers.   In Malaysia, "a small or medium industry" is defined as "a manufacturer with up to 2.5 million ringgits in owners equity." In Japan, a small or medium industry may have up to ¥100 million in owner's equity. Environments   with   unlike   histories   and   public   policies   shape entrepreneurship differently.

> *The best plan for one year is to cultivate grain; that for ten years is to cultivate trees; and that for a hundred years is to cultivate people. Once cultivated, grain may bring about a crop within the year; trees may bring about benefits lasting for a score of years; people may bring benefits lasting a hundred years.*
>
> – Guanxi

Chapter 2

Entrepreneurship in Pacific Asia

The East

The East is a career.
> – Benjamin Disraeli, Prime Minister of England

The concept of "Asia" originates from the ancient civilisation of Mesopotamia and the eastern shores of the Mediterranean Sea. In Assyrian, *asu* means "east." It is likely that ancient Greek entrepreneurs adopted the term from Phoenician merchants, thus designating the land to the east. That was probably between 600 and 500 BC.

The Greeks cultivated relations with Asians, and trade expanded considerably. Both land and sea routes were further developed under the Romans, but mostly to the Indian sub-continent. The Venetian explorer, Marco Polo, wrote accounts of his 13th century travels to India, China, and beyond. However, his contemporaries took little notice. Before the arrival of the Europeans, there were many independent empires in Asia – at least a dozen in south-east Asia alone.

Beginning in the 16th century, European colonialism began to impose a new economic structure, and new patterns of trade emerged. Coffee, rubber and tea plantations were introduced. These being labour-intensive, workers were imported, thereby causing significant demographic shifts and changing ethnic distribution. Whereas Asia had formerly exported finished products, the colonies became exporters of raw materials and importers of manufactured goods. The emphasis on cash crops caused a move away from traditional self-sufficiency.

5

Under British Rule, Baghdadi Entrepreneurs Built Mansions in Penang

The mid-twentieth century saw a return to independence. In 1944, the Japanese declared Indonesia independent, effective at the termination of the war. The independence of the Philippines was declared on July 4, 1946. Ho Chi Minh declared Vietnam independent, on September 2, 1946. Laos, which was declared an associate state of the French Union in 1949, was granted full independence in 1953. Also in 1953, Cambodia declared its independence, which was recognised in 1954. Malaya became independent in 1957. Singapore obtained self-government from the United Kingdom in 1959, and independence from Malaysia, in 1965. However, nations continued to be influenced by their historical experiences.

Cultural and religious differences are also important. Mahayana Buddhists (of the northern school) adopted the name "Greater Vehicle." They called the Theravada (southern) school the "Lesser Vehicle." The state religion in Cambodia is Hinayana Buddhism. In contrast, the principal religion of Vietnam is Mahayana Buddhism. In Malaysia, it is Islam. Singapore is officially multi-denominational, recognising Baha'i, Buddhist, Christian, Hindu, Jewish, Muslim, Sikh, Taoist and Zoroastrian religions.

Asia covers more area than North America, Europe and Australia combined. The geographic focus of this book is the group of east Asian countries neighbouring the Pacific Ocean. These are Cambodia, China, Indonesia, Japan, Korea, Laos, Malaysia, the Philippines, Singapore, Taiwan, Thailand, and Vietnam, collectively Pacific Asia or eastern Asia.

Heterogeneity

Westerners sometimes speak of an Asian model of business or management, without considering the wide divergence within this vast geographic region. Yet, entrepreneurship, today, is shaped by cultural and historical factors. Not surprisingly, peoples with unlike experiences exhibit different approaches to management and entrepreneurship.

The Chinese and Indian minorities in Pacific Asia demonstrated a strong propensity for entrepreneurship. The same is true for Jews from Iraq and also for Armenians. Some chose entrepreneurship because they were unable to integrate into their host society; others did so because cultural values made it socially desirable for them. In other cultures, entrepreneurship is considered to be a less desirable option. Haley and Haley (1998) noted that while merchants are exalted in Japanese culture, they are reviled in Chinese tradition.

Attitudes toward entrepreneurship and entrepreneurs vary not only among countries but also within them. There are important differences among people of one nation. The Chinese, for instance, speak a variety of dialects and different dialect groups have their own clan associations, resulting in unique networks of entrepreneurs with distinct patterns of entrepreneurship. While most Chinese in Vietnam are Cantonese, 77% of the Chinese in Cambodia are Teochew, and 85% of the Chinese in the Philippines are Hokkien (Haley, Tan and Haley, 1998).

The Balinese are more tolerant of Chinese entrepreneurs than are the orthodox Muslims of Sumatra. In Kelantan and in Terengganu (on the east coast of the Malayan Peninsula) pork-eating is not tolerated in public, as this act is considered offensive to the Muslims of this Malaysian province. In contrast, compatibility in religion, social customs and culinary habits allowed Chinese entrepreneurs to integrate easily into Thai society.

A characteristic which reappears across Pacific Asia are the entrepreneurship networks, which bind together entrepreneurs, based on trust. Numerous enterprises work together as a team, with little concern about core competencies. Group conformity prevails over individualism, and relationships prevail over constraints. The entrepreneurship networks transcend the limits of a small-scale enterprise.

Redding (1990) focused on Chinese enterprise – prominent in Pacific Asia. The economic dominance of Chinese entrepreneurs often led to tensions. In response to ethnic discrimination, Chinese entrepreneurs often chose to have a low profile. Rather than develop their own brands, they usually preferred to act as subcontractors, wholesalers and retailers.

The following twelve chapters shall survey entrepreneurship in each of twelve economies. As will be shown, there is no one best approach to entrepreneurship. Rather, different nations adopt policy models, which are relevant to their respective history and culture.

©1999 by Leo Paul Dana

Chinese Entrepreneurs in Laos

©1999 by Leo Paul Dana

Entrepreneurship in the PRC: A Complement to the Socialist Economy

Chapter 3

The Kingdom of Cambodia[1]

Introduction

Cambodia covers 181,035 square kilometres. It lies on the Gulf of Thailand, bordering Thailand, Laos and Vietnam. Cambodia is among the least developed countries in the world. Traditionally, the people of Cambodia – known as Khmers – were not inclined to become entrepreneurs, as entrepreneurship was not seen as contributing to society. An entrepreneurial class developed after independence, but during the 1970s, the Khmer Rouge – officially the Democratic Kampuchean Party – extinguished entrepreneurship in this country. Although private property has been legalised again, a culture of entrepreneurship is not proving easy to reinstate.

Historical Overview

About 2,000 years ago, much of that which is Cambodia today belonged to the Kingdom of Funan – a prosperous nation frequented by merchants travelling between India and China. At the time, Mahayana Buddhism flourished alongside the religion and culture of the Hindus.

During the sixth century, people from the middle Mekong seceded and established their own country, Chenla. These people were associated with

---

[1] The author researched this chapter in Cambodia. Various interviews contributed greatly to the chapter. These were conducted with a variety of individuals, including entrepreneurs, government decision-makers, and representatives of the United Nations Transitional Authority in Cambodia (UNTAC). The Ministry of Finance also provided unpublished data.

Kambu, a figure of Indian mythology and the nation became known as Kampuchea, a derivative of *Kambu-ja* – those born from Kambu.

The country soon expanded and took over Funan. During the Angkorian period (9th to 14th century), the civilisation stretched into today's Vietnam, Laos and Thailand. Indravarom, who ruled from 889 to 910, built an elaborate irrigation system. Jayavaram VII, who ruled from 1181 to 1201, built a new capital – Angkor Thom. (*Angkor* means "the city," in Khmer, while *Thom* means "large.")

During the thirteenth century, the nation gave up Hinduism, in favour of Hinayana Buddhism. Sanskrit was also abandoned. During the fifteenth century, Thais occupied Angkor, and a new capital was built at Phnom Penh. Chinese entrepreneurs built a fine Chinatown there. In 1596, the Spanish arrived and destroyed the Chinese neighbourhood.

The Portuguese modified *Kambu-ja* to *Camboxa*. The French adapted it to *Cambodge*. When anglicised, the name became "Cambodia."

During the early nineteenth century, the ethnic Khmers tended to be attracted to occupations related to agriculture, civil service and monastic life. Commerce and industry were occupations that were left to ethnic minorities. Muslims controlled the cattle trade, commercial fisheries and the weaving industry. The ethnic-Chinese engaged in international trade and in retailing.

King Norodom, who ascended to the throne in 1860, signed a treaty with the French Empire of Napoleon III, in 1863, at which time Cambodia became a French protectorate. In contrast to the adjacent area – corresponding to southern Vietnam – which had its status changed to that of a colony and its alphabet changed to the Latin one, Cambodia had relatively little Occidental influence. Cambodia retained its monarchy and its script. In 1904, King Norodom was succeeded by King Sisowath, who reigned from 1904 to 1927, followed by King Monivong, who died in 1941 under Japanese occupation. Prince Sihanouk was 18, when he was crowned, in 1941.

After the Japanese surrender, in 1945, France made Cambodia an autonomous state within the French Union. In 1953, the *Royaume du Cambodge* (Kingdom of Cambodia) declared its independence, which was recognised in May 1954, by the Geneva Conference.

In 1969, the United States began bombing suspected communist camps in Cambodia. The population of Phnom Penh was slightly more than half a million at the time.

In 1970, Cambodia was agriculturally prosperous but Sihanouk was deposed, with American support, and he moved to Beijing. The country was renamed the Khmer Republic. On April 30, 1970, American and South Vietnamese troops attacked. During the following years, hundreds of thousands of people were killed, and many fled from rural areas to Phnom Penh. In 1975, the capital city was home to 2 million people.

On April 17, 1975 the Khmer Rouge, a group whose goal was to transform the nation into an agrarian peasant-dominated Maoist co-operative, overran the republic. Under the leadership of Saloth Sar – more commonly known as Pol Pot – the Khmer Rouge banned currency and changed the name of the Khmer Republic to Democratic Kampuchea. Millions of city dwellers were ordered to evacuate their homes and to migrate to the countryside; they were duped into believing that these measures were being taken in order to avoid bombings by the United States.

© 1999 by Leo Paul Dana
Lush Vegetation Overran Abandoned Homes in Phnom Penh

Cambodians interviewed by the author explained that the Khmer Rouge communists slit the throat of their prisoners, in order to save ammunition. Women's nipples were removed with pliers, and victims were left to scorpions.

Border clashes between the Khmer Rouge and the Vietnamese led to an invasion by Vietnam on December 25, 1978. On January 7, 1979, Vietnam toppled the Khmer Rouge regime. Again, the name of the country was changed, this time to the People's Republic of Kampuchea. People were once again permitted to reside in towns. Since the urban landlords had been killed by the Khmer Rouge, Phnom Penh was a desolate ghost town at the time. Nevertheless, it was quickly populated as anybody could claim whatever property they wished, on a first come, first serve basis. People returned to Phnom Penh, but infrastructure was lacking.

© 1999 by Leo Paul Dana
Mother Washing Child on Sidewalk

Rice fields were abandoned as masses flocked to urban areas. Famine followed. During the 1980s, the USSR and Vietnam contributed food to Kampuchea.

In September 1989, Vietnam withdrew its troops, and the State of Cambodia was established. However, the Khmer Rouge kept a hold of gem-rich lands neighbouring Thailand. Civil war lingered on. Agriculture was slowly privatised.

As rumours spread that currency might be banned again, people dumped riels to buy gold. The currency, which traded at 190 riels per US dollar in August 1991, tumbled to 830 riels per dollar two months later.

In 1991, the United Nations brokered a peace accord known as the Paris Agreement, which was signed in October that same year. Nevertheless, the Khmer Rouge continued fighting in the jungle, and in January 1992, riots broke out in Phnom Penh. Between mid-July and mid-August 1992, the riel fell by more than 30% against the US dollar. Retailers and even government ministries began refusing local currency. Inflation, in 1992, exceeded 100%, while per capita GNP was $150 US. Government employees were earning monthly wages equivalent to $3.30 US (at the official exchange rate, or $2.56 at the black market rate); not surprisingly, they accepted sideline opportunities.

In 1993, the nation reverted to being a kingdom and Norodom Sihanouk was crowned king, once more. While GDP grew 7% that year, inflation was 55%. In 1994, inflation fell to 26%, but fighting escalated. The US dollar traded at 2,400 riels. The literacy rate was 35%.

Although the Khmer Rouge continued to control its stronghold, economic growth approached 5% in 1995. Per capita GNP was $215.

During the first weekend of July 1997, a coup overthrew Prince Norodom Ranariddh, then Prime Minister of Cambodia. The nation had been scheduled to join the Association of South East Asian Nations (ASEAN) – along with Laos and Myanmar – on July 23. However, on July 10, the members of ASEAN decided to postpone admitting Cambodia into the association. The last Khmer Rouge fighter surrendered in December 1998.

On April 30, 1999 Cambodia officially joined ASEAN. The other members were Brunei, Indonesia, Laos, Malaysia, Myanmar, the Philippines, Singapore, Thailand and Vietnam.

Horse-Cart Near Impromptu Stall in Phnom Penh

Public Policy

Under colonial rule, Cambodia's public policy was dictated by France, which was actually more interested in neighbouring Vietnam. Taxes raised in Cambodia were used to develop southern Vietnam. In Cambodia, the French left the economy to market forces. Across the country, large-scale rubber plantations – which belonged to Europeans – imported workers from Vietnam, justifying this by a claim that the local people were less productive. At the time, Cambodia, Laos and Vietnam used the same currency, making such "imports" very feasible.

French control ended with the independence of Cambodia. The *Banque National du Cambodge* (National Bank of Cambodia) introduced the local currency – the riel, which was pegged to 23.3905 mg. of gold.

In the 1955 elections, the *Sangkum Reastr Niyum* (People's Socialist Community) won every seat in parliament. Although socialist policies were introduced, about 80% of the farmers remained the proprietors of the land which they farmed. Most of the farmers cultivated rice, and many raised animals. In urban areas, the ethnic-Chinese controlled the economic sphere. Seventy-seven percent of these were Teochew Chinese from Guang Dong.

Sihanouk introduced his first economic plan in 1956. It was a two-year plan, the budget of which the United States paid 57%, China 23% and France 17%. Only 3% of the budget was raised by Cambodia. The two-year plan emphasised the role of capital, but ignored private investment and entrepreneurship. The plan was renewed for another two years, beginning in 1958. After that, the Planning Ministry began to set longer plans. The first of these covered the years 1960 to 1964. In 1963, private banks were nationalised and austerity measures resulted in many tariffs being doubled. A new economic plan covered the period 1964 to 1968 and another the years 1968 to 1972.

In April 1975, the Khmer Rouge implemented an unprecedented policy reform, with the goal of transforming the country into a peasant-dominated, agrarian co-operative. During the last two weeks of April, the Khmer Rouge evacuated Phnom Penh, forcing every urban resident out of the city and into slave-labour camps in the countryside.

The regime proclaimed 1975 as Year Zero. Private property, in theory and in practice, ceased to exist. Banks were closed, currency was abolished, postal service ceased to exist, and the regime killed at least one million[2] Khmers (out of a national population of about 7 million), eliminating intellectuals, landlords, entrepreneurs and the business sector. Market activities were banned and all commercial transactions were outlawed. Individuals were allowed only two items of private property, namely a bowl and a spoon. The urban areas, including the capital city, Phnom Penh, were depopulated and would remain empty for over three years. All flights to and from Democratic Kampuchea were halted – except a fortnightly flight linking Phnom Penh with Beijing. The regime designed a four-year plan for the period 1977 to 1980. In 1977, people were required to participate in communal cooking and eating, as Pol Pot banned the private ownership of pots and pans.

When the Khmer Rouge regime was defeated in 1979, trade resumed, but there was no national currency. Commerce relied on barter or foreign money. Only in March 1980 was currency reintroduced, and then only within the context of a socialist economy. Cigarettes, condensed milk, kerosene, rice, soap and sugar were subsidised by the state, but goods were rationed.

---

[2] Vietnamese sources claim the figure to be 3 million.

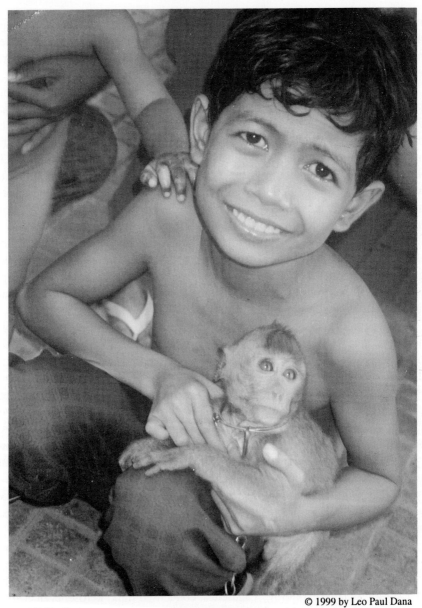

Prize Possession

During the 1980s, the government devalued the Kampuchean currency. In 1984, $1 US bought 7 riels; by the end of the decade, $1 US was worth 380 riels.

Since the 1989 withdrawal of the Vietnamese, the State of Cambodia abandoned socialism, in favour of free-market economic principles. The local authorities divided farmland and distributed it to those living on it. In the urban areas, the Law of Private Ownership allowed persons to claim title to property occupied, and even to sell it.

In August 1991, the National Assembly passed the Law on the Management of Exchange, Precious Metals and Stones. This legislation contained 20 articles governing foreign exchange, precious metals and gems. In November, this law was supplemented by the Foreign Exchange Decree.

By 1992, three quarters of the economy was in private hands. Entrepreneurs were required to pay a signage tax and as a result, many merchants – including prominent retailers in Phnom Penh – opted to have no sign.

© 1999 by Leo Paul Dana

Shops With No Signs

Some entrepreneurs operated from their homes, while others lived in their shops. Smaller-scale vendors set up impromptu stalls. Petrol was sold on roadsides, in used soda-pop bottles.

© 1999 by Leo Paul Dana

Gasoline for Sale in Soda-Pop Bottles

A new constitution came into effect in 1993. Article 56 specified that the kingdom would have a market economy.

In an attempt to improve the inadequate infrastructure, in November 1993, the kingdom participated in the formation of Royal Air Cambodge, to supplement the operations of state-owned Kampuchea Airlines. Royal Air Cambodge was established as a joint venture, 60% owned by the government and 40% by a Malaysian affiliate of Malaysia Airlines (MAS).

In August 1994, liberal laws were implemented to encourage entrepreneurship in the kingdom. A problem, however, was that a very lenient implementation of public policy allowed latent corruption to persist.

Special zoning laws were introduced in 1994, to limit development in the area of Siem Reap; only small-scale ventures were allowed near Angkor Wat, and large hotels were required to be 4 kilometres away. Nevertheless, entrepreneurs could bribe officials and obtain exemptions. In 1997, an article (Desjardins, 1997) in the French daily *Figaro* dubbed Cambodia the "Kingdom of Corruption."

The Nature of Entrepreneurship

Entrepreneurship in Cambodia developed rapidly after independence from France. In 1955, there were 650 small and medium-scale factories in Cambodia. By 1968, there were almost four thousand. Most entrepreneurs, however, were not industrialists. Many were speculators who tried to make fast money in alcohol, beef, gold, land, tobacco, salt and other commodities. These people also contributed to economic instability.

The economy collapsed during the era of the Khmer Republic, which lasted from 1970 to 1975. Manufacturing declined due to shortages of inputs. The republic financed its deficit by printing money and imposing a 60% Value Added Tax (VAT) on cigarettes.

In May 1982, a *National Geographic* essay (White, 1982) reported on entrepreneurs dealing in contraband goods smuggled to Kampuchea from Thailand. These included cigarettes, medicines, soap and watches.

A decade later, the *Far Eastern Economic Review* ran a cover story (Chandra and Tasker, 1992) describing the widespread activities of Thai entrepreneurs who were extracting gems from Cambodia.

In 1995, the *Washington Post* described Cambodia as a "pre-emerging market." That same year, *Paris Match* reported that prostitution was Phnom

Penh's leading industry, with 10,000 prostitutes in town and another 10,000 elsewhere in the country. The prominent French magazine explained that virgins were rented for 2,500FF before being discounted to 200FF. While opium was worth 150FF per gram, a bag containing 200 grams of cannabis cost 10FF. (Marijuana is legal, and commonly added as a flavouring, in soups.)

Meanwhile, some entrepreneurs made 6-year old children work in factories. Other children became entrepreneurs themselves, taking advantage of arbitrage opportunities, selling food and drinks to long-distance travellers on boats, buses and trains.

In 1997, an article (Desjardins, 1997) in the French daily *Figaro* described how government employees in Cambodia were selling, for personal gain, rubber and wood which belonged to the state, in addition to medicines donated by foreign parties, and meant for free distribution.

© 1999 by Leo Paul Dana
Future Entrepreneurs Next to Impromptu Stall in Phnom Penh

On March 7, 1999, the *Japan Times* ("Bear Market" p.11) described poverty-driven Cambodian entrepreneurs dealing in rare animals and their products. In Phnom Penh, an entrepreneur offered an endangered sun bear for sale, for $600US.

© 1999 by Leo Paul Dana

Young Entrepreneur Roasting Corn

Toward the Future

Today, most enterprises in Cambodia are privately held.   However, entrepreneurship is concentrated in grey or black market areas. Casinos and shady banks are said to launder money. Drugs are traded openly.

The historical experience of this nation makes immediate gains more attractive than waiting for an uncertain future, and entrepreneurship in Cambodia is largely short term in nature, due to high risks and uncertainty. People use a young tree for firewood, as they are impatient to wait seven years for it to produce rubber. A more long-term orientation would be desirable in the future.

© 1999 by Leo Paul Dana

Distribution in Downtown Phnom Penh:
Blocks of Ice Delivered by *Cyclos*

The acquisition of values related to sustainable long-term entrepreneurship – such as asceticism, frugality, thrift and work ethic – will take time. The establishment of a solid legal framework of ownership and the rule of law will be prerequisites.

©1999 by Leo Paul Dana

Houseflies Sampling Rice at the Market

Chapter 4

The People's Republic of China (PRC)[3]

Introduction

The People's Republic of China (PRC) – commonly referred to as mainland China, or simply China – covers 9.6 million square kilometres, neighbouring Russia, Mongolia, Kazakhstan, the Kyrgyz Republic, Tajikistan, Afghanistan, Pakistan, India, Nepal, Bhutan, Myanmar, Laos, Vietnam, and North Korea. Unlike the situation prevailing in Cambodia and in other states, which have abandoned communist ideology in favour of capitalism, entrepreneurship in the PRC is merely a supplement to the socialist economy.

While *guoying qiye* is the Chinese term to describe a collective enterprise, *siying qiye* is defined as a private enterprise owned by entrepreneurs and providing employment for 8 or more people. Smaller firms, with fewer than 8 people are referred to as *geteihu*.

---

[3] The author researched this chapter in the PRC. Transportation to the PRC was provided courtesy of United Airlines. Information was obtained from a variety of sources, including: the China Council for the Promotion of International Trade (CCPIT); the China Individual Labourers Association; the China International Trust Investment Co. (Beijing); the Department of Science & Technology for Rural Development; the Economic Management School of Shanghai University of Technology; the Industrial and Commercial Bureau; Kunming Foreign Economic Relations and Trade Commission; the Ministry of Agriculture (particularly its Department of Township Enterprise); and the Ministry of Foreign Economic Relations and Trade, Market and Trade Development Division.

Traditional Shops in Suzhou

Typical Barbershop

Historical Overview

It was over 4,000 years ago that the Xia dynasty – China's first – was established. The society was based on slavery. Much later, in 221 BC, the first emperor of the Qin dynasty – Qin Shi Huang – united China, centralised his authority over the nation, and banned slavery, in favour of feudalism.

The early apex of feudal society, in China, coincided with the Han dynasty. Innovation was encouraged, and during that time China contributed the armillary sphere and the seismograph to the world. It was during the Han dynasty that agriculture, handicrafts, ship-building and weaving were developed. Exhibit 4.1 summarises Chinese history according to dynasties.

Era	Period	Economy
Xia Dynasty (Hsia)	2205 BC to 1766 BC	Slavery
Shang Dynasty	1766 BC to 1122 BC	Slavery
Western Zhou Dynasty	1122 BC to 770 BC	Slavery
Spring & Autumn Period	770 BC to 476 BC	Transition
Warring States Period	476 BC to 221 BC	Transition
Qin Dynasty (Ch'in)	221 BC to 206 BC	Feudalism
Han Dynasty	206 BC to 220 AD	Feudalism
Wei Dynasty	220 to 265	Feudalism
Jin Dynasties	265 to 420	Feudalism
Southern & Northern	420 to 589	Feudalism
Sui Dynasty	590 to 617	Feudalism
Tang Dynasty	618 to 907	Feudalism
Five Dynasties	907 to 960	Feudalism
Song Dynasties	960 to 1279	Feudalism
Yuan Dynasty (Mongol)	1279 to 1368	Feudalism
Ming Dynasty	1368 to 1644	Feudalism
Qing Dynasty (Manchu)	1644 to 1911	Feudalism
Modern	1911 to 1949	Bourgeois
New China	1949 to 1978	Communism
Contemporary	1978 to date	Open-Door & Reform

Table 4.1. Historical Periods in China

The first Westerner to sail into China's Pearl Delta was Captain Jorge Alvares, in 1513. There, he found Guangzhou (Canton), a great trading city. In 1553, officials in Guang Dong accepted bribes from the Portuguese who wished to conduct trade in Macao.

When the Portuguese discovered that the Japanese were willing to buy Chinese silk but that the Celestial Empire prohibited business dealings between Chinese and Japanese merchants, Portuguese entrepreneurs prospered as middlemen between the two.

In 1557, China allowed Portuguese merchants to establish homes and warehouses in Macao. The Portuguese supplied ivory from Africa and cotton from Goa (India) as well as cannons, clocks and mirrors from Europe. In exchange, Chinese entrepreneurs bought porcelain, seed pearls, and silk.

Exporting silk from Macao to Japan proved to be highly profitable for the Portuguese entrepreneurs who were happy to be paid in silver. They then used the silver to pay for Chinese goods, which they sold in Europe.

During the 1600s, entrepreneurs from England decided to get silk and tea directly from China. A problem, however, was that Chinese consumers neither needed nor wanted anything from England. This obstacle was resolved when Chinese entrepreneurs gave English traders silver in exchange for opium from India. The silver was then used to acquire silk and tea in China. Thus, the circle of trade went on and on.

In 1821, the English began using Hong Kong as a base for opium vessels. In 1839, England launched the Opium War against China. Then, Portugal seized Coloane and Taipan from China. In 1841, England occupied Hong Kong Island, and in 1842 the Treaty of Nanking ceded Hong Kong to England. In 1860, Queen Victoria also acquired the Kowloon Peninsula and in 1898 leased the New Territories for a period of 99 years.

In 1887, Portugal forced China to sign the Draft Agreement of the Sino-Portuguese Meeting. This was followed by the Sino-Portuguese Treaty of Peking, allowing Portugal perpetual administration of Macao.

In 1911, overseas Chinese entrepreneurs financed Dr. Sun Yat-Sen's bourgeois-democratic revolution, which overthrew the Qing dynasty. A decade later, the Communist Party of China was established. From 1927 to 1937, the Agrarian Revolutionary War took place. Then came the War of Resistance against Japan, from 1937 to 1945. When Hong Kong fell to the Japanese, many Chinese entrepreneurs fled from occupied Hong Kong to China.

©1999 by Leo Paul Dana
The Peace Hotel, formerly the Sassoon Building, in Shanghai

©1999 by Leo Paul Dana
The Hong Kong & Shanghai Banking Corporation Building

In 1945, capitalists in western China declared the independence of the Turkestan Republic. However, after the National Liberation War (which lasted from 1945 to 1949), Turkestan was absorbed into the newly created People's Republic of China. In contrast, Taiwan went its own way. Entrepreneurship in the PRC was eliminated.

In 1978, Deng Xiaoping set the PRC on the road to liberalisation, with an open-door policy. By the early 1990s, growth peaked at an annual rate of 13.4%.

The All-China Federation of Industry and Commerce – a non-governmental organisation with more than 80,000 members – established its Information Centre in 1995. Its major functions are:

- To provide assistance to foreign entrepreneurs, in finding Chinese partners for joint ventures;
- To perform market analysis;
- To provide consulting services to foreign entrepreneurs;
- To organise trade shows;
- To organise technology exchanges; and
- To assist foreign entrepreneurs.

The federation also publishes periodicals of interest to entrepreneurs.

In 1997, domestic growth in the PRC slowed down, and in 1998, the state responded by launching an elaborate programme of government spending on infrastructure.

Public Policy on Entrepreneurship in China

Chinese entrepreneurship developed without institutional support from the state. Rather than foster entrepreneurship, several emperors attempted to discourage the activities of entrepreneurs. In 1424, Emperor Hung-hsi of the Ming dynasty banned foreign expeditions, and Emperor K'ang-hsi of the Qing dynasty also banned travel. Traditional Chinese law – influenced by Confucian principles – forbade merchants from wearing nice clothes in public. The law also forbade them from riding on horses or wagons.

During the early years of the PRC, the Communist Party of China replaced entrepreneurship with state production and the co-operative system. In 1979, the State Council of China officially endorsed a policy allowing entrepreneurship to contribute to economic development, not as a replacement of central planning, but rather as a supplement to the socialist economy. Regulatory reform legalised entrepreneurship, and by 1980, there were over 1 million entrepreneurs in China.

The government also recognised "specialised households." These were families who were given permission to operate family businesses. Enterprises included animal-husbandry, carpentry, construction, embroidery, and fish-farming. Self-employed farmers were permitted to cultivate apples, beans, corn, grapes, pears, persimmons, rice, sorghum, soya beans, sugar beets and tangerines.

The Chinese proverb, *"A single spark can start a prairie fire,"* led to the term "Spark Programme," referring to an important scheme which was launched in 1986, to promote entrepreneurship in rural areas of China. Through the "Spark Programme," the State Science and Technology Commission encouraged the establishment of several thousand new ventures. Special incentives were offered to entrepreneurs who harnessed a technology deemed to be appropriate for rural industry. This has included enterprises involving agriculture, aquaculture, food processing, light industry, textile manufacturing, and the production of components.

In 1992, the Fourteenth National Congress of the Communist Party of China proposed the establishment of a socialist market economy. In 1993, the China Council for the Promotion of International Trade hosted a world conference in Beijing to encourage entrepreneurship. Devaluation of the renminbi in 1994 helped Chinese entrepreneurs increase their competitiveness in export markets. The state also introduced a variety of incentives for entrepreneurs who export. This included tax exemptions and easy access to financing via specialised banks.

In 1995, legislation declared 339 cities and counties open areas in which entrepreneurship could thrive, as a supplement to socialism. The Financial Security Law came into effect in October 1995. This legislation affected entrepreneurship inasmuch as it covered different forms of security: deposit, guarantee, lien, pledge and mortgage. Land-use rights and social facilities were placed on the list of assets that could be mortgaged.

Until April 1996, foreign entrepreneurs benefited from Value Added Tax (VAT) exemptions and exemptions from customs duties on imported capital equipment. These were subsequently withdrawn, thus putting foreign and local entrepreneurs on equal footing with regards to investment incentives.

©1999 by Leo Paul Dana

Family Business in Shanghai

In 1998, the State Economic and Trade Commission of China was restructured such as to include a Department of Small and Medium Enterprises.

From a high of 43% in 1997, average tariff rates have been reduced to around 17%. It should be clarified, however, that imports are also subjected to VAT. In contrast, local entrepreneurs are often exempted from GST. Thus, it may be said that the effective tariff rate is close to 40%, thereby protecting local entrepreneurs.

©1999 by Leo Paul Dana

The Shanghai Customs House, Protecting Local Entrepreneurs

Making Popcorn in Wu-Xi

Special Administrative Regions of China

In 1984, the Sino-British Agreement pronounced the reversion of British Hong Kong to China, effective July 1, 1997. This was conditional on the PRC creating a Special Administrative Region, conforming to the concept of "One country, two systems." Basically, Hong Kong reverted to Chinese rule, but the Special Administrative Region of Hong Kong was allowed to keep its own legal and judicial system, as well as its capitalist economy (until 2047).

©1997 by Leo Paul Dana

One of the Last Rickshaws in Hong Kong

Along the same lines, in April 1987, Portugal signed the Joint Sino-Portuguese Declaration and Basic Law. This allowed the PRC to take back Macao, on December 20, 1999.

There are, nevertheless, important differences between Hong Kong and Macao. Although both were built on entrepreneurship, their industrial sectors evolved differently. Entrepreneurs in Hong Kong benefit from the government's laissez-faire policy, including favourable tax treatment. In contrast, beginning in 1981, Macao adopted an increasingly interventionist approach.

Hong Kong has at least 300,000 small and medium enterprises, which are flexible, and cost-effective. While their product mix is increasing, the typical size of an order is shrinking.

Many entrepreneurs in Hong Kong are concentrated in the service industries. Others have manufacturing plants, outside Hong Kong. Entrepreneurs from Hong Kong have financed over 170,000 joint ventures in China, and these employ some 10 million people (twice the labour force in Hong Kong). According to unpublished sources at the Hong Kong Trade Development Council, two fifths of the exporters in Hong Kong have operations in two or more economies.

©1999 by Leo Paul Dana

The Star Ferry Linking Hong Kong Island with the Kowloon Peninsula

Double Decker Tram in Hong Kong:
Part of the World's Largest Unsubsidised Public Transit System

The Trade Development Council has a new SME Service Centre in Hong Kong. This is a one-stop shop for entrepreneurs in search of information on technology acquisition and internationalisation.

In contrast, entrepreneurs in Macao tend to be small-scale producers of low-technology goods. These include artificial flowers, ceramics, clothing, electrical products, electronics, firewood, footwear, furniture, machinery, optical devices, plastic goods, textiles and toys. Dana (1999c) provides a detailed contrast of differences between entrepreneurship policy and practices in Hong Kong and those in Macao.

Toward the Future

Although Beijing maintains a tight control of the economy, entrepreneurs – foreign and local – are playing an important role in the PRC's social and economic development.   Heavy   investment   by   overseas   Chinese entrepreneurs has contributed to Guang Dong's economic success.

©1999 by Leo Paul Dana

Workmen Painting Advertisements

In different provinces, entrepreneurship takes on local flavours. In Xinjiang, a Muslim Uygur sells *nan*, a flat bread with *plov* (rice mixed with religiously prepared halal mutton), along with *shashlik* (halal mutton broiled on charcoal). On another street, Han entrepreneurs sell tofu, noodles, dumplings, dogmeat, fried vegetables, white rice and eggs cooked in tea.

Across the PRC, entrepreneurship has become a supplement to socialism and industrialisation is viewed as a complement to agriculture. Unlike other nations, which rapidly abandoned communism, the PRC is liberalising its economy while avoiding spiral inflation. As well, its township enterprises are helping the nation industrialisation while avoiding uncontrolled urbanisation. In the longer term, sustained growth will likely require privatisation of state enterprises and a free flow of labour.

©1999 by Leo Paul Dana

Selling Food in Beijing

Chapter 5

The Republic of Indonesia[4]

Introduction

Comprised of 13,667 islands, Indonesia is the world's largest archipelago. Its total land area is 1.92 million square kilometres. Entrepreneurs, here, are concentrated in labour-intensive industries where the use of traditional methods result in a competitive edge. Popular sectors include clothing, foodstuffs, footwear, furniture, leather, metal products, pottery and wooden products. Most manufacturing takes place in small-scale establishments.

The Central Bureau of Statistics, in Jakarta, defines small industries as units of production using five or more workers, but less than twenty. More traditional are the cottage household industries – units with up to four people, usually family members. Officially, entrepreneurs are required to obtain a basic business permit, *Surat Izin Untuk Perusahaan*. However, there are hidden costs involved, as civil servants often require an abusive bribe before issuing a permit. Therefore, it is common for entrepreneurs not to have one. When officials come around and hassle them, cigarettes and cash are used to avoid fines. Thus, it is easy to function without a permit, but as

---

[4] The author researched this chapter in Indonesia. Courtesy transportation to Indonesia was provided on Japan Air Lines. The chapter is based on information obtained from: the Capital Investment Co-ordinating Board; the Central Bureau of Statistics; the Department of Co-operative and Small Entrepreneur Guidance; the Department of Commerce; the Department of Industry and Trade; the Directorate General of Small Industries; the Institute for Economic Studies, Research and Development, the Ministry of Finance; the Ministry of Co-operatives, the Ministry of Tourism, Post and Telecommunications; and the National Agency for Export Development.

noted by Parnwell & Turner (1998), without one, it is impossible to obtain institutional credit.

Indonesia has introduced a unique special guidance scheme to assist entrepreneurs. The state identifies clusters of entrepreneurs in the same economic sector and in the same geographic region. The clusters – *sentras* – are provided with training, facilities and subsidies.

©1999 by Leo Paul Dana
Selling with a Smile but No Permit

©1999 by Leo Paul Dana

Sifting Peppers at the Market

Historical Overview

The original people of Indonesia were short and dark-skinned. About five thousand years ago, Indians and Malays arrived. Buddhism was brought from India, almost two thousand years ago. When merchants spread Islam to the region, Hindus who resisted Islam moved to Bali.

During the fifteenth century, the Portuguese came in search of spices. Then the Dutch arrived and established the Dutch East India Company, in 1602. The Dutch created the Netherlands East Indies, which they governed between 1799 and 1942. The Portuguese kept eastern Timor until 1975.

In contrast to the British who tried to dissolve the caste system of India, the Dutch opted to develop relations with the Indonesian elite. Descendants of Javanese royalty were invited into the civil service.

Under Dutch rule, Indonesia had three classes. Dutchmen were in control of the higher levels of public administration, as well as the banks and large-scale enterprises such as the Royal Dutch Shell Company. The Indonesians were farmers, and some had small-scale businesses. The Chinese were traders and money-lenders.

©1999 by Leo Paul Dana

Jackfruits, Pineapples, and Pomegranates

Making a Marginal Living

Prior to the Depression, a small number of large-scale merchants prospered. During the 1930s, peasants turned to cash crops. Eventually, the market was saturated with micro-traders, each one making a marginal living.

In 1942, Japan took over Indonesia. In 1944, Japan proclaimed that Indonesia would become independent once the war ended, and independence was formally declared after the Japanese surrendered in 1945. The Dutch attempted to reinstate their imperial government, but the United States threatened to cut off Marshall Plan assistance to the Netherlands, unless the Dutch let go of their former colony (excluding the western portion of Papua New Guinea). In 1949, Sukarno led Indonesia to independence, and became the first president of the republic.

In 1963, Indonesia annexed the western portion of Papua New Guinea, calling it Irian Jaya. Unlike other Indonesians, the people here are primarily Papuan.

A failed coup by communists, in September 1965, was followed by a blood bath. Thousands of Chinese Indonesians were slaughtered in 1966.

In 1967, General Soeharto took the place of Sukarno. That year, Indonesia became a founding member of the Association of South East Asian Nations (ASEAN). The other founding members were Malaysia, the Philippines, Singapore and Thailand. In 1976, Indonesia annexed formerly Portuguese Timor.

During the 1980s, non-tariff barriers were converted to tariffs, and tariff rates were lowered. Financial services were deregulated. Income tax rates and property taxes were reduced. In 1989, foreign direct investment was freed from most controls. In 1990, $1 US bought 1,828 rupiahs (Rp).

A political patronage system, under Soeharto, allowed nepotism and corruption to thrive. Soeharto gave the flour monopoly to his friend Liem Sioe Liong. In partnership with Soeharto, Chinese entrepreneurs controlled 70% of the private sector. The gap between rich and poor widened. Street peddlers were fined Rp1,000, or imprisoned, for operating at road junctions. In 1992, the collapse of Bank Summa shook confidence in the banking sector.

The rupiah tumbled during the financial crisis of 1997. From its level of Rp 2,450 per US dollar in July 1997, it fell to Rp 16,500 in January 1998. Devaluation led to inflation.

Angered over increases in the prices of milk and rice, in January 1998, Indonesians looted stores reported to be charging excessive prices. Shops owned by Chinese entrepreneurs become the focus of aggression. This happened in several Javanese towns, including Jember, Kragan and Losari. On February 13, in Pamanukan (Java), about 600 people attacked every store owned by Chinese entrepreneurs. The rioters hurled stones at some shops and burnt others down, using cooking oil.

By March, prices for food staples had risen by as much as 300% in local currency. In April, seven banks were closed down. These were: PT Bank Centris International; PT Bank Deka; PT Bank Hokindo; PT Bank Kredit Asia; PT Bank Pelita; PT Bank Subentra; and PT Bank Surya. In May, the prime lending rate rose from 36% to 45%, and more price increases led to new riots in Bandung (Java) and Medan (Sumatra). On May 12, looters ransacked Jakarta. *Newsweek* reported that 4,940 buildings were damaged. According to Reuters, damage affected 4,168 stores, 383 offices, 24 restaurants, 13 public markets, 12 hotels and 9 service stations. Riots, in Solo (Java), prompted 600 ethnic-Chinese families to move away. Following the 80% plunge in the value of the rupiah, many foreign parties were reluctant to honour letters of credit that had been issued in Indonesia.

Soeharto was forced to step down in May 1998, and his vice-president, Dr. Bacharuddin Jusuf Habibie began to lead Indonesia out of the Asian Crisis. Nevertheless, the economy contracted by about 4% in 1998, while inflation approached 80%. In 1999, much attention was shifted to ethnic fighting on eastern Timor, where separatists clashed with federalists. Finally, it was resolved that the 1999 national elections be followed by a referendum on the future of self-rule in Timor.

Ethnic Diversity

As indicated in Table 5.1, the population of Indonesia is quite diverse. On the island of Lombok (east of Bali and west of Sumbawa Island), people practice a unique form of Islam, called *Wektu Telu;* followers retain many animist or spiritualist beliefs. Entrepreneurs from Nusa Tenggara dominate towing services. Further west, entrepreneurs from Tegal, on the island of Java, have a reputation for being in the food business; many own street-side food stalls – known as *warung tegal* or *warteg* – catering to low income people. Even further west, Bataks from North Sumatra are clustered in the sale of oil products and the servicing of vehicles.

Madurese entrepreneurs are famous for owning satay stalls. Ethnic Chinese entrepreneurs from Pontianak (west Kalimantan) are traders in building materials. Across Indonesia, the Chinese minority has been successful in entrepreneurship. Chinese entrepreneurs dominate distribution networks for food and other essentials.

Province	Area in sq. km.	Population (Millions)	Pre-Crisis Per Capita GDP Million Rps	Dominant Ethnic Group	Political Climate
Aceh	55,000	4	3.2	Muslim	Separatism
Bali	5,000	3	2.2	Hindu	Stable
Bengkulu	19,000	2	1.3	Muslim	Stable
Central Java	34,000	30	1.3	Muslim	Riots
C. Kalimantan	153,000	2	2.3	Muslim	Stable
East Java	48,000	34	1.6	Muslim	Riots
E. Kalimantan	202,000	3	8.6	Muslim	Stable
East Timor	14,000	1	3.0	Christian	Separatism
Irian Jaya	421,000	2	3.0	Melanesian	Separatism
Jakarta	600	10	6.7	Muslim	Riots
Jambi	53,000	3	1.2	Chinese	Stable
Lampung	35,000	7	1.0	Muslim	Stable
North Sumatra	72,000	12	2.0	Muslim	Riots
Nusa Tenggara	20,000	4	0.8	Muslim	Stable
Riau	94,000	4	4.6	Chinese	Stable
S. Kalimantan	37,000	3	1.6	Muslim	Stable
S. Sulawesi	72,000	8	1.1	Muslim	Riots
South Sumatra	103,000	8	1.8	Muslim	Stable
West Java	43,000	40	1.5	Muslim	Riots
W. Kalimantan	146,000	4	1.7	Chinese	Stable
West Sumatra	50,000	5	1.7	Chinese	Stable
Yogyakarta	3,000	3	1.6	Muslim	Riots

Table 5.1. Ethnic Diversity in Indonesia

© 1999 by Leo Paul Dana

Ethnic Diversity in Indonesia

©1999 by Leo Paul Dana

Vendor in Riau Province

The Chinese in Indonesia

During the 1800s, the Dutch welcomed Chinese traders in Indonesia, and used Chinese entrepreneurs as business partners. Thus, the success of ethnic-Chinese entrepreneurs in Indonesia dates back to the *Vereenigte Oost-Indische Compagnie* (United East Indies Company), which granted them monopoly leases. Later, the Dutch colonial government did the same, further contributing to the economic success of Chinese entrepreneurs on these islands. Even when the monopoly leases were phased out, at the end of the nineteenth century, former lease-holders continued trading.

By 1900, there were 227,000 ethnic-Chinese in Java and another 310,000 on other Indonesian islands. They included self-employed artisans, builders, contractors, furniture-makers, manufacturers, money-lenders, repairmen, shippers, shopkeepers, smiths, speculators, suppliers, and tanners; they owned abattoirs, gambling dens, grocery stores, pawnshops, real estate and warehouses.

As explained by Kahin (1952), sharp trading practices used by aggressively competitive Chinese entrepreneurs contributed to the rapid growth of *Sarekat Dagang Islam* after 1909. This propagated anti-Chinese sentiment, and by 1912 anti-Chinese riots were a reality in Surabaya and Surakarta.

The twentieth century saw demographic and social changes among the Chinese in Indonesia. Fluent in Dutch, the children of established families strayed away from their family businesses, and drifted toward salaried professions. The more recent immigrants did not integrate into the established community. Many newcomers became peddlers or low-wage labourers. This caused an increasing gap between the existing Indonesian Chinese and new arrivals from China. During the 1920s, however, many Chinese wage-workers became small-scale merchants. By 1930, according to the census of that year, there were 1,230,000 Chinese residing in Indonesia.

Among the Chinese immigrants who arrived in Indonesia, in 1938, was Liem Sioe Liong. During the 1950s, he befriended an army supply officer, who later became President Soeharto. Through his Salim Group, Liem Sioe Liong became Indonesia's most successful entrepreneur, with 300 companies producing cars, cement, chemicals, cooking oil, flour, milk, noodles and steel.

During the rule of Sukarno (1945-1966) anti-Chinese pressure prompted 119,000 ethnic-Chinese people to leave Indonesia. Those who stayed were prohibited from being entrepreneurs in rural areas. The rational was that indigenous Indonesians should have a chance to be merchants. Under Soeharto, the Chinese were barred from government office and most professions. The lack of alternatives encouraged them to concentrate their efforts in the commercial realm.

The Soeharto regime adopted a policy favouring the indigenous Indonesians – known as *pribumis*. These people were entitled to favourable credit terms, and they had easy access to permits. Indonesians could acquire permits, and they did. Then, they sold them to Chinese entrepreneurs, with immense mark-ups.

Unlike the Indonesians who have traditionally used time as a limitless commodity, Chinese entrepreneurs in Indonesia come across as more focused. Meetings have a purpose beyond social gatherings. The Chinese in Indonesia are motivated by profit.

In June 1998, there were about 7 million ethnic-Chinese in Indonesia. This represented 3.5% of the country's population. Yet, ethnic-Chinese entrepreneurs owned 70% of the private sector in Indonesia.

In September 1998, ethnic-Chinese entrepreneurs controlled 170 conglomerates in Indonesia as well as 5,000 medium-sized firms and 250,000 small enterprises. According to Yeung (1999), the overseas Chinese controlled 80% of corporate assets in Indonesia in 1999. Although the Chinese in Indonesia adopted Indonesian names, they never fully integrated with the indigenous population. Half of Indonesia's Chinese are Hokkien.

Culture and Entrepreneurship in Indonesia

Penujak, on the island of Lombok, is home to potters who use the *turun temurun* method of making pottery. Since the 1500s, this skill has been passed on from mother to daughter, using no tools other than a round stone and a wooden paddle.

In Sukhara, a village of 3,000 people, also on Lombok, about 600 families are self-employed weavers. The men grow cotton and the women weave it into cloth, which is sold in larger towns, such as Sweta. Families also grow cloves, coffee, garlic, rice, soya beans and tobacco for personal use.

Indeed, many indigenous Indonesians are self-employed, inasmuch as they are subsistence farmers. However, market-oriented entrepreneurship is not central to the culture here. In Javanese, the word for trader also signifies "tramp," or "foreigner."

In contrast, the ethnic-Chinese, in Indonesia, thrived in entrepreneurship. One causal variable may be their culture, but it should also be emphasised that they were given few alternatives, as they were barred from many other occupations open to indigenous Indonesians. By the same token, indigenous Indonesians complained that ethnic-Chinese entrepreneurs also created barriers to entry.

As ethnic-Chinese entrepreneurs became increasingly successful in Indonesia, Javanese would-be-entrepreneurs complained that Chinese entrepreneurship was a de-facto barrier to entry, inhibiting the Javanese from becoming self-employed. The Chinese had more experience in business, more capital, better networks, and international contacts.

During the 1950s, new legislation prevented the Chinese from living in certain towns. This included the locally-born Chinese (Peranakans), as well as ethnic-Chinese immigrants (Totok). The objective was to give a competitive advantage to the indigenous *pribumi* people. Customs regulations also prohibited the import of Chinese medicines and/or printed matter in Chinese characters. The next section addresses public policy in Indonesia.

Public Policy on Entrepreneurship

At the National Level

President Sukarno, who ruled from 1945 to 1966, introduced anti-business policies to Indonesia. For instance, the Land Reform Bill of 1960 redistributed property; individuals were limited to 7½ hectares, the equivalent of approximately 19 acres.

Beginning in 1969, Indonesia implemented a series of five-year national development plans. These typically emphasised development in rural areas. The first two plans focused on agriculture.

©1999 by Leo Paul Dana

Indigenous *Pribumi* in Native Attire

In 1973, Indonesia introduced the Small Enterprises Development Programme (SEDP). This was a subsidised credit scheme to help cottage industries and small-scale indigenous enterprises controlled by *pribumis*. The SEDP was discontinued in January 1990.

The Third Five-Year Plan (1979-1984) began giving assistance to clusters of similar types of small firms – known as *sentras*. These will be discussed in a separate section.

The Fourth Five-Year Plan (1985-1989) established a framework for the development of national industry. Among the plan's objectives was finding solutions for major problems facing small-scale entrepreneurs, namely financing, marketing and technical problems.

As the price of oil dropped, Indonesia deregulated large sectors of its economy. In October 1988, Indonesia launched important bank reforms, which reduced capital restrictions.

The Fifth Five-Year Plan (1989-1994) emphasised entrepreneurship and the development of small industries. The plan called for tripling private sector investment in targeted industries, including agriculture and tourism. The plan focused on small-scale and household industries, especially those outside urban areas. In January 1990, the SEDP was replaced by the *Kredit Usaha Kecil* (KUK), an unsubsidised credit scheme.

The Directorate General of Small Industry was created (within the Ministry of Industry) with the purpose of financing the new ventures of competent entrepreneurs. The *Kredit Investasikecil* – the government's small-scale investment credit scheme – made it possible for small-scale industries to obtain capital for the purpose of purchasing fixed assets. As well, *Kredit Modal Kerja Permanen* – the permanent working capital credit scheme – allowed firms to receive working capital loans, through banks, at subsidised rates. Also, the (central) Bank of Indonesia started a Small Enterprise Development Project, the purpose of which was to train loan officers and to simplify lending procedures.

In October 1989, policy changes allowed foreign entrepreneurs to have 100% ownership of an enterprise in the Batam Economic Zone, for a period of five years. Also, private firms were permitted to set-up industrial estates.

During the 1990s, the banking sector was liberalised, but Soeharto asked banks to increase lending to small firms. Until 1992, the seven state banks of Indonesia operated along sectoral specialisation:

- Bank BNI met the needs of manufacturers and traders;
- Bank Bumi Daya served plantations;
- Bank Dagang Negara focused on mining;
- Bank Exim did import-export financing;
- Bank Pembangunan Indonesia specialised in finance for transport;
- Bank Rakyat Indonesia financed farmers; and
- Bank Tabungan Negara mobilised public savings.

In 1992, reforms blurred the distinction between different banks. Indonesia's new Banking Law was passed in February 1992, and in August, Indonesia's seven major state banks became joint stock enterprises. This was a move away from bureaucratic regulations and toward profitability. A problem with this restructuring, however, was that it became expensive for entrepreneurs to borrow capital. Also in 1992, the Directorate General of Small Industry adopted an official policy of promoting entrepreneurs who employed between five and nineteen workers. Since then, the Directorate General has focused on helping entrepreneurs with marketing, production and financing problems.

In 1995, the government passed Small Business Law Number 9. This act led to the National Partnership Programme.

The Sixth Five-Year Plan focused on the development of small enterprises in 2,200 villages. Indonesia amended import duties, effective January 1996. On fish, duty rates ranged from 0 to 25%.

In 1996, the National Agency for Export Development began reporting to a recently enlarged ministry. The agency included centres for export information, promotion and product development.

Provincial Efforts

The provincial governments and the provincial offices of the (federal) Ministry of Industry jointly implement a Small Industries Development Programme, the *Program Pembinaan dan Pengembangan Industri Kecil*, commonly referred to as BIPIK. Unlike the federal credit programmes, BIPIK provides no capital. Instead, it contributes technical assistance.

Under the wing of BIPIK, the Directorate General of Small Industry got involved in the *Bapak Angkat-Mitra Usha* (Foster Father Business Partner) linkage scheme, to assist, finance, train and facilitate marketing for entrepreneurs. This involves a large "Foster Father" firm and a small business partner, both entering in a symbiotic, co-operative agreement. Several thousand large firms have signed co-operation agreements with tens of thousands of small business partners across Indonesia.

Provinces also have their own development programmes. The island province of Bali, for instance, has carefully formulated economic and social objectives, which bridge the gap between village life and commerce. Emphasis is on agriculture and small-scale industries, as well as tourism. Indonesia is the world's principal supplier of vanilla, and 85% of Indonesia's vanilla is grown in Bali. Farmers on this island province also produce cashew nuts, cinnamon, cocoa, and coffee. In addition, women in Bali raise pigs, which are exported live to Singapore. As well, Bali is a regional exporting centre for canned tuna fish. Although Indonesia exports tin, a commercial beef-canning facility closed when it could not obtain tin-plate for its cans.

International Entrepreneurship

Indonesia has relaxed restrictions on foreign direct investment, allowing a foreign entrepreneur 100% ownership of a firm in the industrial and services sectors. The Capital Investment Co-ordinating Board – locally known as BKPM – oversees such enterprises. Restrictions are published in the Investment Negative List – locally called the DNI – listing businesses for which foreign ownership is restricted. Approved entrepreneurs may be entitled to exemption from import duties and to postponement of Value Added Tax (VAT), in addition to unrestricted international movement of funds.

Non-Governmental Assistance to Entrepreneurs

In Indonesia, not only the state, but also large firms have programmes to assist entrepreneurs. A motivating factor is that once assisted, entrepreneurs often become subcontractors, suppliers and/or distributors for the assisting firm. This results in sophisticated vertical integration.

In 1980, PT Astra International established the Dharma Bhakti Astra Foundation (YDBA) to demonstrate the firm's commitment to the Small to Medium Scale Enterprise and Co-operative Reinforcement Programme. The foundation's mission is to assist entrepreneurs in production techniques, processes, financing, management, and marketing. The YDBA began providing on-the-job training for entrepreneurs, and many of these became sub-contractors for PT Astra International. Just prior to the Asian Crisis, 243 foundation-assisted firms were subcontractors, while 224 served as suppliers and vendors for multinationals.

Other non-governmental organisations, which assist entrepreneurship in Indonesia, include the Association for the Promotion of Small Enterprises and the Indonesian Chamber of Commerce & Industry. In addition, the Institute of Management Education and Development provides training for entrepreneurs.

Sentras

Sentras are clusters of similar small-scale enterprises in the same line of business and in geographical proximity of one another. These clusters exist in the rural areas of each province, and also in some urban centres, including Bandung, Jakarta, Semarang and Surabaya.

The first clusters occurred naturally. These included the producers of batik in Java and weavers of cloth on several islands. Other clusters were created by government initiatives.

Sentras facilitate the state's task of providing assistance to entrepreneurs. Machinery and technical support – unaffordable by any one firm – are made available for common use, within a *sentra*. In some cases, participating firms also form *kopinkras* – small-scale craft co-operatives – to facilitate procurement of inputs and access to credit; these also strengthen the marketing programmes of smaller firms.

Such networking and co-operation between entrepreneurs has enhanced performance, and competitiveness. Also, the cluster approach has been cost-effective. From the government's perspective, clusters facilitate logistics of assistance, by the state and by state-owned firms such as the electric utility company, PLN.

Clusters of traditional craftsmen include silversmiths in Sumatra and copper specialists in Java. Clusters of wood carvers exist in Bali. Other clusters group together entrepreneurs in the chemical, food, footwear, leather and textile industries.

In contrast to the West, where competing firms tend to be rivals, *sentras* encourage co-operation among different firms in the same industry. Clustering may also facilitate marketing. The geographical proximity of firms – within a cluster – simplifies sub-contracting to firms that require huge quantities of goods.

Toward the Future

When, in 1998, the flight of capital coincided with the exodus of ethnic-Chinese entrepreneurs, this led to economic and social chaos. Chinese entrepreneurs had controlled distribution channels in Indonesia and these take time to be replaced. Government efforts were needed, in order to create a new class of *pribumi* entrepreneurs. In 1999, populist decision-makers were giving loans based on economic need, rather than on entrepreneurship potential. The return on capital will be low, and possibly negative. Critics accused such incidents as attempts to buy votes.

Nonetheless, the *sentra* system and the co-operatives arising therefrom have been successful means by which to assist entrepreneurs in absorbing technology, developing skills and enhancing their marketing abilities.

A problem, however, is that the recent crisis and riots prompted children to drop out of school, becoming street-wise entrepreneurs with short-term goals, but lacking a knowledge-intensive base. Perhaps members of *sentras* can be encouraged to absorb such youths.

The old-style entrepreneurs in Indonesia usually had two or three sets of accounting books: one for personal use, another for shareholders, and yet another for tax purposes. The next generation includes MBA graduates more open to a Western management style. However, it is very likely that corruption will survive into the future. Corruption, common in business and in government, is a reason for which people aspire to be civil servants. Parnwell and Turner (1998) reported that individuals may pay Rp 5 million to obtain such a job, and then spend a large part of their career trying to obtain bribes to make their money back.

Entrepreneurship in Indonesia is in transition. Each year, the Capital Investment Co-ordinating Board (BKPM) publishes a priority list, which targets areas for growth. Entrepreneurs, in desired sectors, may qualify for tax incentives. In addition, the Bank of Indonesia oversees the implementation of credit facilitation to entrepreneurs, while the Directorate-General of Small-Scale Industry contributes technical assistance. The Ministry of Manpower operates an entrepreneurship-training programme, and the National Agency for Export Development assists entrepreneurs to sell overseas. Yet, many would-be entrepreneurs are below the poverty line and not aware of either development programmes or tax incentives.

Chapter 6

Japanese Spirit & Western Knowledge[5]

Introduction

Japan is an archipelago of 3,000 islands, covering about 378,000 square kilometres. *The Economist* reported that the self-employed, and their unpaid family workers, account for nearly a third of the labour force in Japan; this corresponds to Japan having more entrepreneurs per capita than any other big industrial economy. The flagship of entrepreneurship, here, is the sector of *chusho kigyo* – literally, "small and medium enterprises," with an emphasis on smallness. The official definition of *chusho kigyo* is: retail firms with up to 30 employees, wholesale operations with up to 100 employees, or others with up to 300 employees, or with share capital not exceeding 100 million yen. Of 2 million enterprises in Japan, only 1% is considered to be large. About 80% of the workforce is employed by *chusho kigyo*. In the die

[5] The author researched this chapter in Japan. The University of Pittsburgh provided transportation to Japan. The chapter relies on information gathered from: the All Japan Committee of the Association of Small and Medium Sized Enterprises; the Association for the Promotion of Traditional Craft Products of Japan; the Central Federation of Societies of Commerce and Industry; the Institute of Small Business Research and Business Administration at the Osaka University of Economics; the Japan Chamber of Commerce and Industry; the Japan Federation of Smaller Enterprise Organisations; the Japan Small Business Corporation; the Japan Small Business Firm Foundation; the Ministry of Foreign Affairs; the Ministry of International Trade and Industry; the National Association for Subcontracting Enterprise Promotion; the National Federation of Merchant and Industrial Organisation; the National Federation of Small Business Associations; the National Small Business Information Promotion Centre; the New Business Investment Co. Ltd; the Small & Medium Enterprise Agency; the Small Business Information Gathering Promotion Association; the Small Business Investment Company Limited; the Small Business National Corporation; and the Traditional Craft Industry Council.

and mould industry, a firm with 100 employees is considered to be a major producer. Yet, Japan is a country in which a big size is desirable. An old proverb teaches, *"When seeking a shelter, look for a big tree."*

Rather than compete with large firms, entrepreneurs in Japan co-operate with them, serving as suppliers and assemblers, in an intricate relationship revolving around cultural beliefs. Japan has an ancient and intricate cultural tradition, founded on legends, myths and rituals. Central to the Japanese belief system are the concepts of mutual obligation, indebtedness, hard work, self-sacrifice and loyalty, all of which reinforce the very important notion of harmony for the common good. Additionally, in Japan, the individual is always conscious of belonging to a group. Therefore, enterprises also tend to form associations. The concepts of obligation, indebtedness and loyalty contribute to the unity and success within each partnership, and to the harmony among groups.

©1999 by Leo Paul Dana

Working Together in Harmony

Historical Overview

External influences were often responsible for major changes in Japan. Until the ninth century BC, the Japanese were a gathering society who fished and hunted for subsistence. Approximately in the third century BC, the Yayoi era started, and people cultivated rice. The art of farming was introduced from the mainland. Metal tools, such as ploughshares, arrived from Korea, and the development of agriculture led to community life. Hence, villages were settled.

Eventually, with the collapse of the Han dynasty in China, a huge wave of migration was observed all over the archipelago. Thus, the 7th century was typically characterised by the whole range of movements that took place. As the number of Chinese refugees increased, there was a wave of people moving down the Korean Peninsula and up to those that are now considered the Japanese islands.

As movements of people, together with mixes, borrowings and exchanges, increased all through the archipelago and as writing and the Buddhist religion were introduced, inequalities became accentuated and some clans began to enjoy much more power than did others. Out of this situation emerged the Yamato clan, which seemed the most powerful because of its close ties with the Korean court. The latter, in turn, had the closest links with the powerful lineage that was ruling China at that moment, the T'angs. Thus, as time went on, a trend toward private land ownership, by nobility links to the Yamato clan, became increasingly accentuated, especially during the Heian Period. The year 894 AD marked the beginning of Japan's cultural independence from China and Korea.

For the several centuries between 1185 and 1868, Japan continued to have an emperor, but the shogun was the powerful head of the samurai (mercenaries). During the fourteenth century, a civil war was fought over two lines of emperors.

In 1467, the destruction of Kyoto – the capital of Japan, at the time – was an important turning point in history. During the Momoyama Period, from 1573 to 1603, manufacturing and commerce were greatly encouraged, and international trade flourished. (Table 6.1 provides a chronology of Japan.) A concern, however, was that contact with foreigners introduced Christianity and Western influence to Japan, beginning around 1600. In response to this, the principal characteristic of the Edo Period (1603 to 1868) was a severe policy of seclusion. The Japanese were divided, according to the Confucian model, into four distinct social classes – samurai (bureaucrats as well as warriors), then farmers,[6] followed by craftsmen and lastly merchants. This, coupled with efficient government, personified by the shogunate, maintained harmony in Japan.

Ancient or Early Japan	Nara	710-784
	Heian	784-1185
Medieval Japan	Kamakura	1185-1333
	Muromachi	1333-1573
	Momoyama	1573-1603
Early Modern Japan	Tokugawa (Edo)	1603-1868
Modern Japan	Meiji	1868-1912
	Taishô	1912-1926
	Shôwa	1926-1989
	Heisei	1989-date

Table 6.1. Historical Periods in Japan

In an effort to end a period of war, the Tokugawa leaders came up with the Confucius-inspired *Baku-han* policies that divided the empire into various little groups called *han*. The fact that all of these autonomous regions reported directly to the shogun resulted in a total lack of lateral contacts between various *hans*, and in the formation of many dialects. This very totalitarian top-down political system led to the isolation of the archipelago from other countries, because of bureaucratic law. However, it is important to realise that the insulation of the shogunate did not imply ignorance of what was going on in the rest of the world. Rather, information was tightly controlled. For instance, while a group of people was sent abroad to study Dutch medicine, Christian missionaries were crucified because they represented a threat to the shogunate. Consequently, contact with the outside world was to be avoided (in order to limit European impact and influence) and was strictly restricted to the port of Nagasaki, where a limited amount of trade was permitted.

---

[6] These included entrepreneurs who owned their own land as well as peasants who did not.

However, Japan's self-imposed isolation ended when Commodore Perry of the US Navy penetrated Tokyo Bay on July 8, 1853, thus ending Japan's 250 year-long seclusion, and asking for the opening up of Japan to trade with Westerners. In 1868, power was returned from the shogun to the emperor. This was referred to as the Meiji Restoration.

The end of a policy of seclusion, coupled with the Meiji Restoration, would lead to rapid industrialisation, as Japan was faced with the dilemma of whether to form a modern nation or to surrender to colonialism. The government opted to invest heavily in infrastructure and in the establishment of pilot industrial plants in various sectors. These sectors included bricks, cement, glass, machine tools, military needs and mining.

In order to avoid being engulfed by industrialised powers of the West, Japan would need to master the fundamentals of Occidental economics, while rejecting Western culture. Thus, the 1860s are typically characterised by the "opening of Japan" as various revolutions to dismantle the shogunate and its overarching power structure took place. Afterwards, during the first decade of the Meiji era, the doctrine of *bunmei kaika* (civilisation and enlightenment) prevailed. This was characterised by a collective effort to eradicate the past and to modernise, in order to "look" Western. Consequently, not only was Tokyo entirely rebuilt and literally unrecognisable by the end of the 1870s, but the Japanese adopted Western fashions, read Shakespeare and Tolstoy, and many rejected their own language for the sake of adopting English. At the heart of all this was a firm and optimistic belief that enlightenment, science and modernisation would solve everything. Thus, Japan adopted standardised mass production along with imported economic models, but modified them in order to incorporate Japanese cultural values. The motto was *wakon yosai*, which is roughly translated as "Japanese spirit and Western knowledge." However, the *sai* is more than knowledge; it also incorporates skills and wisdom.

The 1880s arrived with a financial crisis, to which the government reacted by privatising some industries. In 1884, the Ministry of Agriculture and Commerce promulgated the Trade Association Regulations, the purpose of which was two-fold: to protect traditional industries and to prevent the mass-production of poor quality goods.

Passing on Traditions

In 1897, the government passed the Law on the Trade Association Dealing with Major Export Products, establishing an association of exporters. However, three years later, this law was repealed, and replaced by the broader Law Regarding the Trade Association Dealing with Major Products. This new law shifted the focus of policy from exporters to manufacturers and marketers of domestic products.

The co-operative association system was launched in 1900, with the Industry Co-operatives Law. In 1914, the Japanese Commerce and Industry Association was established.

In 1920, Japan had only thirty large firms in the machinery sector. In contrast, there were 6,450 small firms (with between 5 and 30 employees), that produced lower quality goods. There was a large gap between the large and the small firms. The preponderance of small, low-precision, engineering firms gave Japan a reputation of being backward in the machinery industry.

The Law on the Chamber of Commerce and Industry was passed in 1927. The Japan Chamber of Commerce and Industry was established in 1928.

In 1931, Japan enacted the Industrial Co-operatives Law and the following year, the Commercial Co-operatives Law legalised the commercial co-operative system. The year 1934 saw the introduction of the Unfair Competition Prevention Law.

During the 1930s, a petition of signatures was collected from people protesting the establishment of department store branches and the spread of department stores in city-centres. As a result, in 1936, the Retail Industry Improvement Investigation Committee resolved "Matters Regarding the Relationship between Department Stores and Smaller Retailers." This led to the Department Store Law, in 1937. The Commercial Retail Store Law followed in 1938. In 1942, the cabinet announced a policy to improve the retail industry.

The Fair Trade Commission was established in 1947. The Small and Medium Enterprise Agency and the Small and Medium Enterprise League of Japan were both established in 1948. That same year, the National Federation Headquarters established the Committee on Promotion Measures for Small and Medium Industries. The Small and Medium Enterprise Agency recommended that local organisations set up counselling offices for entrepreneurs.

In 1949, the yen was fixed at 360¥ per US$. Also in 1949, the Small and Medium Enterprise Agency launched a monthly journal entitled, *Information on Small and Medium Enterprises.* The following year the agency launched a semi-monthly newsletter.

In 1952, the Small and Medium Enterprise League of Japan became the Small Business Associations League of Japan. In 1956, the Small and Medium Enterprise Promotion Council was established.

The Small and Medium Enterprise Basic Policy Council was established in 1962. In 1963, the Institute of Small Business Research was established, at the Osaka University of Economics. In 1967, the Small Business Promotion Corporation was launched.

A Quaint Restaurant in Kobe

In 1981, the Small and Medium Enterprise Agency established the Small and Medium Enterprises' Overseas Investment Advisory Programme. The purpose was to provide advice for entrepreneurs expanding overseas.

The Plaza Accord of October 1985 led to a 50% revaluation of the yen against the US dollar. Rather than increase American exports, this action spurred Japan's export performance. In 1988, Japan's per capita GNP exceeded that of the United States for the first time. In April 1989, the Institute of Small Business Research of the Osaka University of Economics was enlarged to become the Institute of Small Business Research and Business Administration.

In 1991, the Subcontracting Small and Medium Enterprise Working Group of the Small and Medium Enterprise Modernisation Council announced a plan to revise the Subcontracting Small and Medium Enterprise Promotion Law. The so-called bubble economy is said to have burst around that time. Nevertheless, very low interest rates helped the economy recover in 1996.

In April 1997, Japan raised its consumption tax. Immediately, household consumption decreased. Later that year, crisis in Asia spread to Japan. Unemployment rose from 3.5% in 1997 to 4.3% in 1998 – the highest since such data was first compiled in 1953. Real GDP growth declined in the fiscal year ending March 1998. This was the first incident of negative growth since March 1994.

©1999 by Leo Paul Dana

Tekka-Maki

Culture in Japan

Since the Edo Period (1603 to 1868), wholesalers have held an important position in Japan, and this nation still has four times more wholesalers per retailer than is the case in the United States. While the United States has 1.9 million retailers, Japan, with roughly half the population, has 1.7 million retailers. The average product, in Japan, passes through five layers of distribution, more than double that in the United States. Americans may perceive this as inefficient, but for the Japanese, the maintenance of such established relationships is very important. More direct marketing channels would reduce direct costs, but this would destroy the existing harmony, and the reasons for this existing distribution system extend beyond cultural values. Given that Japan is, geographically, a small island nation covered largely by rugged mountains, 70% of the population lies in an area occupying only 20% of the country. The result is densely populated cities, and high real estate prices therein. Consequently, storekeepers save much rent by keeping their shops small. However, such small shops have limited storage space. Similarly, Japanese homes have small kitchens with limited storage space for fresh foods. Therefore, Japanese consumers shop for food on a daily basis. This contributes to high turnover at small neighbourhood shops. To avoid daily stock-outs, these small shops rely on small-scale wholesalers who make frequent deliveries, each involving a small load. Each small-scale wholesaler, in turn, relies on other wholesalers, and the global picture is one of a multi-tiered distribution system, which emerged as a result of complex cultural, political and physical factors.

In 1974, liberalisation strengthened this pattern, with the Large Store Law, stating that no retail outlet larger than 5,400 square feet may be built without the permission of local storekeepers. This barrier to entry helped maintain the status quo, and the complex network of marketing channel survives, with its implicit code of elaborate interpersonal obligations.

Among Japanese cultural obligations is gift-giving. This interaction can increase harmony, and facilitate business transactions. Gift offering is an expected behaviour; in Japan, the art of gift-giving is among one's important interpersonal obligations. There are gifts for all occasions and for many, money is not a concern when presenting an offering. Yet, caution is warranted here, as the wrong gift may be disruptive to harmony. A potted plant must not be presented to a sick patient for fear that an illness may take root. Knowing what is appropriate for every occasion can lessen somewhat embarrassing moments and actually enhance business and personal relationships. Table 6.2 illustrates a gift glossary by identifying the Japanese words associated with the occasion for such offerings.

Ochugen	These are seasonal gifts presented in July, to those to whom one is indebted throughout the year.
Okaeshi	These are "return" gifts, which are presented by recipients of goodwill presents, such as to acknowledge appreciation. Funeral money is thus returned with a gift worth 50% of the original present. Other gifts are returned with *okaeshi* worth 15 to 20% of the value of the original gift.
Omimai	These are gifts presented to those who are ill or recovering from disease.
Omiyage	These are souvenirs, which commemorate a particular journey, such as a business trip.
Oseibo	These are seasonal gifts presented in early winter to those to whom one is indebted throughout the year.
Okurimono	These gifts can be very useful when they are presented to individuals from whom one is requesting a favour.
Oiwai	These are gifts which are presented on occasions of personal celebrations, including weddings.

Table 6.2. Japanese Gift Glossary

Public Policy on Entrepreneurship in Japan

Japan has long been interested in its entrepreneurs. In 1930, the Temporary Industrial Council issued a report on public policy for small and medium industries. The League of Small and Medium Commerce and Industry of Japan was established in 1932. Given the then current economic depression, a relief fund was set-up, in the context of a Financial Relief Programme for Small and Medium Commercial and Industrial Enterprises.

In 1938, the Ministry of Commerce and Industry set up a committee on "Unemployment Relief Measures for Small and Medium Commerce and Industries." Also that year, the ministry established basic policies regarding entrepreneurs, and announced the Plan for Small Industrial Enterprises to Co-operate in Performing Shared Activities.

In 1940, the cabinet established Measures for Small and Medium Commerce and Industries. Later that year, the Ministry of Commerce and Industry circulated a document, *Guidance and Counselling to Help Small and Medium Commerce and Industries with Each Other.* As well, the cabinet announced a new economic system in which entrepreneurs were to flourish and streamline themselves voluntarily.

In 1942, the Planning Agency established the Reorganisation Committee for Small and Medium Commerce and Industries. The cabinet announced the Policy Regarding the Improvement of Small and Medium Industries.

After WWII, Division 1 of the Economy Stabilisation Headquarters created the Committee on Measures for Small and Medium Industries. In 1947, new measures prohibited private monopolies and unfair trading. The government established guidelines for small and medium enterprises assistance.

In 1948, the Small and Medium Enterprise Agency Establishment Law was passed. Also that year, the state established guidelines for small and medium enterprises. Meanwhile, the Finance Restoration Committee established procedures for using funds for the financial reconstruction of small and medium enterprises.

In 1952, regulations were established to govern the registration of consultants to entrepreneurs. In 1954, the state created a subsidy programme for the acquisition of modern equipment. This was regulated by the Guidelines Concerning the Granting of Subsidies for Constructing Common Facilities for Small and Medium Enterprise Co-operative Associations.

In 1955, the Small and Medium Enterprise Stabilisation Law was revised, as was the Law Regarding Co-operative Associations of Small and

Medium Enterprises. Also, the state established a programme for the granting of subsidies to encourage small and medium enterprises to produce goods for export. A minimum wage law was enacted in 1959.

In 1963, the Small and Medium Enterprise Basic Law created the Small and Medium Enterprise Agency, to safeguard the interests of this sector. In 1964, revisions to the Small Business Association Law imposed restrictions on the advancement of large-scale enterprises into the sectors dominated by small and medium enterprises. In 1967, the Organisation of Small and Medium Enterprise Assistance Law was revised, thereby establishing the joint-business co-operatives system.

In 1970, the government enacted the Law on the Promotion of Sub-contracting Small and Medium Enterprise. During the following years, many existing laws were amended. The Small and Medium Enterprise Basic Law was revised in 1973 and again in 1983. In 1993, the state enacted the Law Regarding the Assistance for Small and Medium Enterprises by Societies of Commerce and Industry and the Chamber of Commerce. In 1995, Japan passed the Special Law on Facilitating the Creative Business Activities of the Small and Medium-Sized Enterprise.

©1999 by Leo Paul Dana
Vending Machines Selling Beer, Ice-Coffee & Cola

Although entrepreneurship in Japan may have acquired Western knowledge, it has retained Japanese spirit, including cultural and traditional values such as the sense of obligation, indebtedness and loyalty within business alliances. Public policies help perpetuate this pattern, and across industries, small businesses in Japan are usually linked to a network of one kind or another.

Toward the Future

Since WWII, a few small-scale engineering firms in Japan grew into multinationals. These include Honda and Sony. However, these very large firms were exceptions. The majority of Japanese enterprises specialised in niche activities. For many, the niche was to serve as subcontractor for major enterprises.

This complementarity between small and large firms, coupled with a cultural system of harmony, enhanced the efficiency of the Japanese economy. Small-scale entrepreneurs helped large corporations to prosper, while the latter gave entrepreneurs a raison-d'être as well as a livelihood. Cultural values helped propagate the inter-firm linkages.

Dana (1998a) described the business alliances in Japan. These include: the *keiretsu* (a diversified enterprise group); the *sanchi* (a group of small firms in a similar line of business); the *kyodo-kumiai* (a co-operative of small businesses); and the *shita-uke gyosha* (subcontractors) of the *shita-uke seido* (subcontract system). Such alliance systems can serve as de-facto trade barriers, because loyalty within a network makes it harder for outsiders to penetrate. In difficult economic times, however, financial constraints may strain relationships within alliances.

Japan Air Lines Convair 880

Chapter 7

The Republic of Korea[7]

Introduction

The Republic of Korea – popularly known as South Korea – shares the Korean Peninsula with the Democratic People's Republic of Korea (North Korea). The two Koreas are separated by the Demilitarised Zone (DMZ), a 4 kilometre-wide strip at the 38th parallel.

Prior to the 1945 division of Korea, industry was concentrated in the north, and agriculture in the south. During the three and a half decades during which the Japanese occupied Korea, they built factories, railroads and hydroelectric plants in the north of the country, *i.e.*, the area which became North Korea. In the territory that eventually became known as South Korea, the principal industries were farming and fishing. Given its abundant coal and iron reserves, North Korea was expected to prosper more than its counterpart to the south. However, entrepreneurship was banned in North Korea. Given the constraints associated with conducting field research in North Korea, the focus of this chapter is South Korea.

---

[7] The author researched this chapter in the Republic of Korea. Transportation to Korea was provided courtesy of Air Canada. The chapter relies greatly on information obtained from the Bank of Korea; the Economic Planning Board; the Federation of Korean Industries; the Korea Development Institute; and the Ministry of Trade and Industry. As well, it draws on previously published works by the author.

Historical Overview

Korea was first unified during the seventh century, and the nation prospered under Buddhist culture. The Chosun dynasty, started by General Yi Song-gye in 1392, ruled Korea until Japan abolished the Korean monarchy in 1910.

Under the Yi dynasty, Korea maintained a tributary relationship with China. There was little market activity in Korea. Until the 18th century, monopoly rights protected Korean merchants.

During the 1870s, Japanese traders arrived, and the Japanese yen soon replaced barter trade in Korea. Japanese entrepreneurs also introduced their merchandising methods to Korea.

In 1876, Japan forced Korea to accept a one-sided commercial treaty. China and others did the same. Investment flowed to Korea, from Britain, France, Germany, Russia and the United States, but Japanese entrepreneurs dominated the business realm in Korea.

As foreign traders controlled the Korean economy, the Yi dynasty instituted reforms, but these were not enough, and in 1894 Korean peasants revolted. Chinese intervention suppressed the revolt, but this led to substantial Japanese military presence in Korea.

Following its victory in the Sino-Japanese War (1894-1895) and the Russo-Japanese War (1905), Japan annexed Korea in 1910. From 1910 to 1945, the Japanese treated Korea as a colony. Japan separated the monarchy from the state, codified civil law, outlawed discrimination against commoners and monetised the economic system. The colonisers appropriated 40% of Korea's area, monopolised natural resources, took control of public services and took command of finances.

The educational system was designed to assimilate the Koreans as lower elements in Japanese society. Japanese firms discriminated against Korean employees, and Korean entrepreneurs were unable to compete with Japanese entrepreneurs. This prompted 2 million Koreans to revolt in 1919.

Nevertheless, the harsh military rule obligated the Korean people to produce more and more rice for the Japanese, and to serve as a market for goods manufactured in Japan.

New technologies were introduced as the Japanese invested in irrigation. While the Japanese were countering a rice shortage in their archipelago, Korean farmers starved to death because their entire rice harvest was shipped to the colonising country.

©1999 by Leo Paul Dana

Traditional Roof-Tops of Agricultural Settlement

Eventually, Japan moved from an "agriculture first" policy to one of manufacturing in Korea. The Japanese owned virtually all large-scale firms in Korea, while Koreans had some smaller factories. The number of Japanese companies increased from 109 in 1911, to 1,237 in 1929. In contrast, Korean entrepreneurs owned 27 firms in 1911, and 361 in 1929.

Between 1919 and 1930, Japan implemented a policy to eradicate Korean national identity. The Koreans were forbidden to speak their language. Japan censored the press, and despoiled Korea's resources.

Beginning in 1930, Japan focused on preparing for war. That year, just less than one quarter of Korean factory products went to Japan. Northern Korea was used as a manufacturing base for Japan, while the south provided fish and agricultural produce.

Following the Manchurian Incident (1931-1937), the Japanese decided to industrialise Korea in order to fully take advantage of its mineral resources in the north and of its rice supply. The Japanese needed to build factories, hydroelectric plants and railroads. They needed capital (90% of which came from Japanese conglomerates known as *zaibatsu*), technology (100% of which came *zaibatsu*), and labour (100% of which was provided by poorly paid Korean workers). Consequently, the ratio of light to heavy goods in Korea (which was 80:20 in 1930) became 50:50 during WWII. By 1940, half of Korean factory products went to Japan. This process resulted in the growth of small and medium scale capitalists, the increase of skilled male workers, migration, urbanisation, and the loss of the black and white nationalist outlook which had characterised the Korean people ever since the arrival of the Japanese.

At the end of World War II, Soviet forces took control of northern Korea, while American troops occupied the south. In August 1948, the Republic of Korea (South Korea) was proclaimed. To the north of the 38th parallel, the Soviets created the Democratic People's Republic of Korea (North Korea).

In 1950, North Korea invaded the south, with the aspiration of creating a united communist Korea. An armistice was signed in 1953.

In 1963, Park Chung Hee became the president of South Korea. His policy was to develop the economy of his country. The next section examine his policy for economic development and its impact on entrepreneurship in Korea.

Public Policy in the Republic of Korea

From 1953 to 1961, South Korea received about two thirds of its total investment in the form of rehabilitation aid from the United States. These investments were used to implement an import substitution policy.

A military coup in 1961 initiated a policy of rapid industrialisation. As South Korea accelerated its industrialisation, legislation was introduced to protect entrepreneurs and to help them be productive contributors to the economy. In 1961, the Small and Medium Industry Bank Act designated a financial institution – the Industrial Bank of Korea – to make loans only to small-scale entrepreneurs. Similarly, the Kukmin Bank was mandated to give loans only to enterprises with fewer than 200 employees.

In 1962, when South Korea adopted its first Economic Development Plan (1962-1966), per capita GNP was $82 US. President Park Chung Hee subsequently created a command economy with wages and interest rates at his order. With the objective of maximising growth and export volume, he set wages low and subsidised interest rates.

Several economic development plans helped the president guide the economy. The Second Five-Year Plan (1967-1971) and Third Five-Year Plan (1972-1976) allowed him to encourage exports rather than import substitution. The won was devalued, and financial support was channelled to high performers. Given that market demand interest rates may cause a heavy debt burden on entrepreneurs, and hence decrease the pace of new venture formation while increasing the bankruptcy rate, selected firms in South Korea were granted subsidised interest rates well below the market-clearing point. The low cost of borrowing allowed for the development of capital intensive methods of production over labour-intensive ones, and the excess supply of labour kept wages low, a competitive advantage for exporting.

Thus, instead of helping entrepreneurs at large, President Park Chung Hee specifically used his control over bank credit to channel subsidised loans to export-oriented borrowers. These few exporters soon grew into the debt-based mega-conglomerates known as *chaebols*. Small-scale entrepreneurs were squeezed out of many markets, resulting in numerous monopolies and oligopolies.

The economic effects, of South Korea's Vietnam venture during the late 1960s and early 1970s, went far beyond the simple acquisition of foreign exchange. Many South Korean firms, including Hanjin and Hyundai, got their first big economic boost from the Vietnam War. Korean firms became contractors for the United States army in South Vietnam and later made use of their Vietnamese contacts and experience to expand into the international construction business, most notably in the Middle East. Between 1974 and 1979, South Korea's top ten *chaebols* took home nearly $22 billion (US) in Middle East construction sales, of which Hyundai's share alone was over $6 billion.

In 1974, the Credit Guarantee Funds Act provided guarantees for liabilities of entrepreneurs. In 1975, the Sub-Contracting System Promotion Act promoted co-operation between large firms and smaller ones. The Fourth Five-Year Plan (1977-1981) perpetuated a tight credit policy. Consequently, the national economy of South Korea was based on rapid industrialisation of only very few non-integrated industries – heavy industry and chemicals – for the purpose of increasing exports. Hence, the economy was dominated by a small number of highly diversified mega-conglomerates, resulting in various problems.

©1999 by Leo Paul Dana

Among the *Chaebols:* LG

South Korean industry was largely dependent on foreign suppliers for raw materials and light industry components as well as for machinery and replacement parts which also had to be imported, a drain on the country's financial resources. Therefore, much capital had to be raised in the form of foreign loans, causing a further burden – that of debt service.

As national policy favoured the *chaebols,* these flourished while small business remained small. Although the factories of *chaebols* were efficient, their offices tended to be less so, as considerable time was consumed in meetings as well as bureaucracy. A further problem with *chaebol* administration was the highly hierarchical structure which makes a manager feel very subordinate to an immediate superior, often causing an employee to serve a superior personally instead of concentrating on innovation.

The Small & Medium Industries Promotion Corporation Act, in 1980, provided financial support, technical assistance and managerial consultancy to entrepreneurs. The following year, the Procurement Facilitating Act specified the conditions of government procurements from entrepreneurs. This allowed smaller enterprises to sell to the state, collectively, via co-operatives.

In 1983, the Policy to Support Promising Small and Medium-scale Enterprises provided low interest loans, technical training and management consulting to promising small and medium enterprises. In 1984, the Mutual Assistance Fund Act provided special loans to entrepreneurs. In 1988, the Production Research Institute Act created an institute to assist entrepreneurs with technology transfers and product development.

Prior to the labour unrest of 1989, wages were unrealistically low, a factory worker earning as low as the equivalent of roughly $50 US for a 72-hour week. Wages were subsequently raised substantially. Salaries were 45% higher in 1989 than in 1987, and those in automotive industry climbed 80% from 1986 to 1989 – contributing to price increases, which were already high due to the lack of competition in many monopolistic and oligopolistic markets. Rationalisation, which followed, led to increased unemployment.

In 1989, the government made available credit guarantee funds for technology development among entrepreneurs. Also that year, several commercial banks were permitted to provide services exclusively to entrepreneurs.

Five *chaebols* were producing more than 50% of Korea's GNP. In consideration of this fact, a government priority during the 1990s was to build up small and medium sized firms and to encourage the development of innovative entrepreneurs, with programmes such as capital assistance including low cost loans for new ventures and R&D incentives to facilitate innovation. Government initiatives were designed to encourage:

➢ A general trading company system and the provision of fiscal or commercial advantages;
➢ Commitment by the constitution to foster small business;
➢ Special support for small exporters;

> Direct and indirect financial assistance for small business;
> Commitment by banks to make 35% of their loans to smaller firms;
> Tax concessions for new ventures, particularly those with innovative ideas or using competitive technologies; and
> Facilitation of foreign investment.

In February 1993, a newly elected government issued the 1993-1997 five-year plan. This called for reduced government intervention in the economy, lowering of entry barriers and deregulation of business activities. Tariffs were reduced. Many restrictions on the import of capital goods were eliminated. A special depreciation allowance was introduced for fixed assets. High-tech entrepreneurs were allowed to import capital goods duty-free, and their firms were granted a five-year exemption on corporate income tax. Registration qualifications for trading enterprises were abolished effective 1997.

In 1998, the government established the Corporate Restructuring Fund, with a value of $1.2 billion US, half of which was provided by the Korean Development Bank, and the other half by a consortium of banks, insurance companies and investment houses. Seventy percent of the fund was earmarked for established small and medium firms, especially those focusing on high technology and exports. The top five *chaebols* were banned from borrowing from the fund, and new ventures were discouraged.

Trends

Development of a Domestic Component Industry

The *chaebols* traditionally imported light industry components as well as raw materials. Gradually, foreign suppliers were replaced by the small business sector. The development of one million small and medium-sized businesses in South Korea – diversified in various sectors, including manufacturing, trading, service, transportation, and construction as well as mining – led to increased trade between *chaebols* and small firms providing components.

Exports

The general trading company systems, as initiated by the government, significantly contributed to export volume by small firms. Product and market diversification became prime objectives of the trading companies, resulting not only in short-term profit but also in long-term growth. Small firms began to export labour-intensive light-industry goods, which South Korea previously did not export. Their production also developed component industries within South Korea, thus helping domestic growth and further helping exports indirectly.

Productivity

Until the Asian Crisis, small manufacturers consistently increased their production at a rate higher than that of large manufacturers. Government sources indicate that productivity in South Korea's manufacturing sector improved by an average of 11% per year, while productivity among smaller firms (in the same sector) increased by an annual average of 14%.

Toward the Crisis

The post-1993 financial liberalisation in South Korea encouraged entrepreneurs to obtain short-term loans. Some borrowers opted to borrow abroad. In 1996, the country qualified for admission to the Organisation of Economic Corporation and Development (OECD). However, problems soon emerged. Although *chaebols* had an average debt-equity ratio of 400%, the economy was still healthy in 1997. Growth rate was 5.5%, inflation was stable at 4.4% and unemployment at 2%. A foreign exchange crisis, however, led to an economic crisis.

Korea's meltdown, in November 1997, led the government to seek an International Monetary Fund (IMF) package. The following month, Korea signed a $58 billion IMF bailout. Financially-fragile entrepreneurs faced the domino effects of bankruptcies.

During the Crisis: Selling Peppers on the Street Corner

Toward the Future

The South Korean policy approach, subsidising credit to selected export-oriented firms, resulted in a command economy dominated by *chaebols*. From 1961 to 1967, the government supported *chaebols*, and these generated full employment. *Chaebols* could produce mediocre products in a protected environment and Korean consumers bought their products. Then, tariff reductions made South Korea increasingly open to competition from abroad.

The opening of the economy, coupled with the Asian Crisis, necessitated major changes. As the highly diversified *chaebols* were being trimmed, cost reduction measures released skilled personnel with entrepreneurial potential. Also, product restructuring gave rise to new opportunities for emerging entrepreneurs. Thus, the restructuring of *chaebol* portfolios provided opportunities for entrepreneurship. However, in 1998, 1,000 Korean entrepreneurs were going bankrupt every month. According to unpublished documents at the Bank of Korea, 18 large companies and 5,221 smaller ones declared bankruptcy during the first five months of 1998, compared with 10 and 2,197 during the same period in 1997. Some communities experienced reverse industrialisation, as entrepreneurs gave up industrial production, in favour of agriculture.

©1999 by Leo Paul Dana

Market Scene in Seoul

Chapter 8

The Lao People's Democratic Republic[8]

Introduction

The Lao People's Democratic Republic – also known as Laos – is one of Asia's most undeveloped nations, and among the five poorest in the world. The landlocked country, enclosing 236,800 square kilometres, is nestled between Cambodia, China, Myanmar (Burma), Thailand and Vietnam. Laos is sparsely populated. It is among the least urbanised nations in Asia.

Traditionally, business activities in Laos have not been associated with high social status. Cultural values, stemming from religious beliefs, emphasised instead the elimination of desire. Commerce, on the other hand, is perceived as a means to satisfy desire. Social forces thus discouraged enterprise, and trade has usually been the role of those with inferior social standing.

The communist take-over further discouraged entrepreneurial spirit. The result is a generally non-entrepreneurial society, in which the Chinese community of 67,000 people (1.3% of the population) is very active in the entrepreneurship sector. Large corporations in Thailand, each earn more than the value of all the goods and services produced in all of Laos.

---

[8] The author researched this chapter in Laos, drawing largely from a variety of unpublished sources as well as interviews. Especially helpful was the Ministry of External Economic Relations, in Vientiane.

© 1999 by Leo Paul Dana

The Role of Women is Culturally Determined

Historical Overview

The Lao people are thought to have arrived from China during the eighth century. During the 1200s, Kublai Khan led the Mongols to seize power in China. This prompted further migration to the region that would later become Laos. During the following century, a Khmer empire was established here. It was known as *Lan Xang* – literally "Million Elephants." The Lao people organised themselves into Lao principalities.

During the nineteenth century, France persuaded one of the leaders to accept a French protectorate, as insurance against China and Siam. Then, France united all of the Lao principalities into one country. Thus came to be the name Laos, which is the plural of Lao.

France used Laos as a buffer between French Vietnam and British Burma. The French imposed a Vietnamese-staffed civil service in Laos, but France did not contribute to the protectorate. When the Japanese occupied French Indochina (Cambodia, Laos and Vietnam) in 1941, the Lao people obtained more autonomy than they had experienced under French protection.

Following WWII, the French tried to take back Laos, but in 1949 the latter was declared an independent associate state of the French Union. The United Nations recognised Laos as a separate country, and in 1953 France allowed Laos to become a monarchy.

In December 1975, the Lao Patriotic Front – the political arm of the *Pathet Lao* (Lao People's Party) – abolished the monarchy and created a communist entity, the Lao People's Democratic Republic.

Changing Public Policies on Entrepreneurship

When the Lao People Revolutionary Party took control of the Lao People's Democratic Republic, in 1975, it implemented a policy of accelerated socialisation. Harsh policies shunned entrepreneurship and co-operatives replaced private initiatives. Former royalists were sent to re-education camps where they were forced to accept communism.

In 1987, Laos introduced its New Economic Mechanism. This recognised market forces as legitimate, and began liberalising the centralised economy. The first national election took place in 1989. Two years later, a new constitution ushered in more economic reforms. New laws were subsequently introduced, governing property, labour and foreign investment.

Ushering in Private Reforms

In April 1994, Laos and Vietnam signed an agreement on goods in transit, which allowed these commodities to be transported across either Laos or Vietnam, on the way to the other. It was expected that this would facilitate international entrepreneurship.

In May 1994, Laos introduced a liberal law governing investments. This streamlined foreign investment regulations and tax structures. Legislation included tax holidays, a 1% import duty on capital goods associated with production, and a flat-rate corporate tax of 20%. This was to lead to a major influx of foreign capital to create joint ventures, as well as 100% foreign-owned investments in commerce, industry and services. Furthermore, the government committed itself to expedite the business application process. Japanese and Taiwanese investors expressed considerable interest.

Laos joined ASEAN on July 23, 1997. The geographic position of Laos could help it become an important assembly and trans-shipment centre to other markets in the region.

Goods in Transit

The Traditional Belief System

Laotians are still noticeably influenced by folk tales, superstitions, and the ancient beliefs of the national religion, Theravada Buddhism. An article in the August 28, 1992 issue of *Asiaweek* explained that it is commonly believed that the Mekong River gets "hungry" for human souls, without which the annual rains will not arrive:

> a little girl (was) swept away by the current while picnicking with her family on a sandbank. Her mother and father made no attempt to save her. Two foreigners snatched the child from the swift water after a desperate effort. The parents were fearful because the river had been thwarted in claiming the child (p. 63).

©1999 by Leo Paul Dana
Main Street in Vientiane: The Mekong in the Background

Across Laos, Theravada monasteries, known as wats, dominate every town, while almost every house, shop and office has a private temple. It is even common for boats, cruising the Mekong River, to dock for the crew to jump ashore, light incense and pray. The Lao wats are architecturally distinct from monasteries elsewhere in Asia. In Laos, wats have large terraces, and flare symbols on the roofs.

Theravada monks are highly influential in Lao society. They are consulted on virtually all matters, thereby playing an important role in a diversity of spheres, ranging from private life to government policy. They have traditionally had a great impact on the educational system; it used to be that the only schools were in wats.

Buddhism is Central to Life in Laos

Monks are Central to Lao Society

The official calendar used in Laos is that of the Lao Buddhist era (not to be confused with the Thai calendar); the Christian year 2000, for example, corresponds to 2638 in the Lao calendar, and 2543 in the Thai calendar.

Central to Theravada beliefs is the ultimate goal to extinguish unsatisfied desires. Its doctrine focuses on aspects of existence, including *dukkha* (suffering from unsatisfied desire), and *anicca* (impermanence). Assuming that unsatisfied desires cause suffering, then suffering can be eliminated if its cause (desire) is eliminated. A respectable person, then, according to this ideology, should not work towards the satisfaction of materialistic desires, but should, rather, strive to eliminate the desire itself. A monk, for instance, is specifically prohibited by the religion, from tilling fields or raising animals.

Lao folk tales reinforce the belief that a male monk should not labour for material wealth; yet, the same folklore conditions women to accept a heavy burden in exchange for honour, protection and security. Even the Lao currency portrays agricultural work being done by women.

Numerous Lao families who farm during the wet season become self-employed gold-diggers during the dry season. Prospectors camp along the Mekong River, especially in the region of Luang Prabang. The women do the heaviest work, digging for dirt and panning it in wooden trays. The men weigh the gold, up to one gram per day.

In a 1994 article entitled "Indochina," the *Far Eastern Economic Review* (May 5, 1994) quoted a London newspaper as saying that "Lao rice farmers have a reputation in this dynamic region for lying down, closing their eyes and listening to their crops grow in fertile paddy fields (p. 60)." It is very true that entrepreneurial spirit is not very prevalent in the traditional Lao belief system. Dana (1995d) addressed this issue in detail.

The Entrepreneurship Sector

Given the traditional belief system of Laos, the small business sector here consists largely of foreigners. Most restaurants, movie theatres, hotels, repair shops and jewellery shops in urban areas are owned by ethnic-Chinese. Some Chinese entrepreneurs, who were interviewed by the author, claimed to be descendants of entrepreneurial families who established themselves in Laos several generations ago. There are at least 2,500 ethnic-

Chinese in Vientiane – most of them Teochews – and they tend to be entrepreneurs.

Muslim men are also involved in the small business sector of Laos. Individuals from India and Pakistan are especially active in the garment industry.

In addition, Thai and Australian entrepreneurs have recently created numerous new ventures in Laos. Unlike the Chinese and the Muslims who reside in Laos permanently, the Thais and Australians in Laos tend to be sojourners.

Whereas United States involvement in Lao business tends to be in the form of large business (24 projects worth $82.5 million US in 1994), Thai investments tend to be in the medium-size category (167 investments valued at $198 million US in 1994), as are Australian ventures (29 enterprises worth $29.4 million). More involved in small business are French entrepreneurs, with 42 ventures costing $17.8 million.

One problem encountered by entrepreneurs in the manufacturing sector is the poor infrastructure. Given the generally poor conditions of the roads (often flooded during the rainy season) and the lack of a railway, a quarter of all traffic in Laos uses the Mekong River. People and buffalo stand side by side, on boats or barges, for hours. Sometimes, cargo gets damaged.

A gift from the people of Australia, the $30 million (US) Friendship Bridge across the Mekong River between Laos and Thailand was opened in 1994, with the hope that it would facilitate international trade.

As for the Lao people, 85% are involved in agricultural sectors. Crops include coffee, corn, rice, tea, tobacco, vegetables and wheat. Given that three fifths of the GNP comes from agricultural output, the government has instituted reforms providing incentives to farmers. The plan introduced preferential agricultural tax policies, increasing agricultural investment, especially in irrigation. It also raised the prices of agricultural produce, and linked remuneration with output.

Per capita rice output in Laos is 350 kg. Nevertheless, some provinces experience occasional rice shortages. Many farming communities are migrational, deforesting land for a crop, and then moving elsewhere. There is a constant breeze of smoke and ashes over the Mekong River. Opium is an important crop, of which Laos produces about 300 tons annually.

©1999 by Leo Paul Dana

Nurturing Friendships

On the Road to the Future

Toward the Future

Government reforms have increased the autonomy of firms, and the state no longer has the monopoly on supply, purchasing and marketing. Yet, entrepreneurship is still limited in Laos, as the culture does not encourage it. Entrepreneurs tend to be women or foreigners. The local shortage of skilled labour limits manufacturing. Furthermore, the shortage of educated individuals limits the service sector.

©1999 by Leo Paul Dana
Three Generations at the Market

Chapter 9

Malaysia[9]

Introduction

Located between Indonesia, Singapore and Thailand, Malaysia occupies 332,633 square kilometres. It covers the Malayan Peninsula and it shares the island of Borneo with Brunei Durussalam and Indonesia.

Under colonial rule, British administrators encouraged indigenous Malays to work the land, while the ethnic-Chinese dominated the entrepreneurship sector in Malaya. Since independence, government efforts have been trying to change this, by formulating ethnic-based policy to govern entrepreneurship in Malaysia. Nevertheless, the Chinese minority – comprising approximately 30% of the population – still control a disproportionate amount of capital assets in this country. Chinese entrepreneurs own most small firms in Malaysia.

Historical Overview

Ancient remains suggest that the original Malays came from south-western China. These people were invaded by the ancestors of today's Malays.

---

[9] The author researched this chapter in Malaysia. Courtesy transportation to Malaysia was provided on Japan Air Lines. The chapter draws on information obtained from: the Agricultural Bank of Malaysia; the Central Bank of Malaysia; the Credit Guarantee Corporation; the Development Bank of Malaysia; the Labuan Offshore Financial Services Authority; the Malaysian Industrial Development Authority; the Ministry of Finance; and the Ministry of Trade and Industry.

In 1402, Prince Parameswara of Sumatra founded Malacca, on the west coast of the Malayan Peninsula. In 1405, Emperor Yung-Yo, of the Ming dynasty created favourable relations between China and Malacca. Chinese traders came to the Malayan Peninsula and this attracted merchants from distant places. Malacca thrived as a port-of-call for entrepreneurs from China, India, and Arab lands. The trading centre was home to Bugis, Chettiar, Chinese, Gujerati, Javanese, Mon, and Tagalog Muslim entrepreneurs who prospered in the entrepot trade. In Malacca, cloves and pepper were exchanged for western textiles. Some entrepreneurs on the Malayan Peninsula dealt in minerals, rice and teak in addition to cloves and pepper. In time, these traders developed a sophisticated network, which included entrepreneurs in Burma and Sumatra.

Portugal used its colony on the Indian sub-continent, Goa, as a base from which to set off to Malaya. In 1511, the Portuguese conquered Malacca, but the Dutch defeated them, in 1641. The Dutch introduced monopolistic practices and disrupted the traditional commercial patterns of local entrepreneurs. The Mons abandoned their long distance trade routes. The indigenous trading networks collapsed, and by 1681 Malay entrepreneurs gave up their trade with China, India, Japan, Persia, the Philippines, Siam and Vietnam. Although the Dutch imposed a 20% duty on Chulia entrepreneurs, the Chulias kept their lead in the textile trade.

To the dismay of the Dutch, in 1786, the British East India Company expanded to Penang. In 1795, Malacca was given to the British. In 1824, the Anglo-Dutch Treaty gave Bencoolen (a British post) and the rest of Indonesia to the Dutch, while the British were allowed to control Malaya and Singapore. In 1826, the British created an entity, which they named the Straits Settlements, under the jurisdiction of the British East India Company, in Calcutta.

The British East India Company controlled the Straits Settlements until the demise of the company, in 1858. The settlements then came under the control of the India Office, in London. In 1867, they were transferred to the Colonial Office, as the Straits Settlements became a Crown Colony. At the time, the Straits Settlements consisted of Penang, Malacca and Singapore. In 1874, the Islands of the Dindings were added to the colony.

©1999 by Leo Paul Dana
Remnant of Dutch Colonial Times

For the convenience of the British, the Cocos Keeling Islands were attached in 1886, followed by Christmas Island in 1900 and the Island of Labuan in 1906. For administrative purposes, the colony was divided into four settlements:

- The Settlement of Singapore (including the Island of Singapore, the Cocos Islands and Christmas Island);
- The Settlement of Penang, including the Island of Penang, Province Wellesley, and the Territory and Islands of the Dindings;
- The Town and Province of Malacca; and
- The Settlement of Labuan (off the coast of Borneo).

Small-scale rubber production gained popularity in the early 20th century, as there were virtually no barriers to entry. The industry required minimal capital and this was readily available. According to Drabble (1973), by 1921, 37% of the total rubber acreage in Malaya belonged to small-scale entrepreneurs. This corresponded to one-eighth of the total world production of rubber. However, many Malay entrepreneurs lost their plantations to Chettair money-lenders from southern India. This led to the Smallholdings Restriction of Sale Enactment, in 1931.

©1999 by Leo Paul Dana

Money Lending in Malacca

Small Scale *Bumiputra* Landholding

The Straits Settlements were dismantled in 1946, just months after the Japanese surrender. Also in 1946, the British territories on Borneo were re-organised such that North Borneo (Sabah) and Sarawak became two separate colonies. That same year, the British also forged the Malayan Union, consisting of Malacca and Penang, along with the nine existing Malay states. These were Johor, Kedah, Kalantan, Negeri Sembilan, Pahang, Perak, Perlis, Selangor, and Terengganu. The union was dissolved in 1948 when the states of the Malayan Peninsula formed the Federation of Malaya, which became independent in 1957. Having lost its free-port status, Penang's importance as a trade centre declined during the 1960s.

In 1963, Malaya joined Sabah, Sarawak, and Singapore to create a new kingdom, Malaysia. However, tension escalated between the ethnic-Chinese and the Malays. In 1965, Singapore was expelled from the union. Yet, there continued to be Chinese people in Malaysia and they became the victims of racial riots.

©1999 by Leo Paul Dana

Looking for Business in Penang

The Ethnic-Chinese in Malaysia

Most Chinese immigrants to Malaya did not come as entrepreneurs. During the nineteenth century, labourers left China to work in the mines of Malaya. Their passage was usually sponsored by an entrepreneur, who became entitled to be their exclusive employer for a period of one year.

When they docked in Malaya, the newcomers (*sinkeh*) were taken by armed guards, to their place of employment. There, they were locked up at night. The employees were virtual prisoners, until they had paid back their debt, at which time they were promoted from *sinkeh* to *laukheh* – literally "old hand."

"Secret societies" were the principal organisations of Chinese immigrants. Chinese entrepreneurs – *towkays* – were the leaders of these societies and they controlled their employees through these societies.

©1999 by Leo Paul Dana

The Chinese Established Banks & Medicine Halls

©1999 by Leo Paul Dana

The dominant society in Kuala Lumpur was the Hai San, led by Hakka entrepreneurs. Hokkien entrepreneurs developed an important rice network, importing rice from Burma and elsewhere, milling it in Malaya and exporting it to Hong Kong and beyond. According to the *Straits Settlements Trade Commission's Report,* rice imports to Penang reached 213,648 tons in 1918. In time, the Straits Chinese, known as the Baba and Nyonya, adopted many Malay traditions.

Today, Chinese entrepreneurs own most small-scale industry in Malaysia. At least a third of them were born in China, and their firms generally have a low level of capitalisation. Expansion is not common, and many firms remain sole proprietorships. The Hokkiens are the largest group of Chinese in Malaysia (one-third of the Chinese population) and the prominent Chinese dialect federation in the country – with 138 affiliated associations – is the Federation of Hokkien Associations of Malaysia. The federation developed its own business arm, with investments in China as well as Malaysia.

Three Scripts on Storefront

Public Policy

The British colonial administration, in Malaya, encouraged a marked division of economic roles, along ethnic lines. Indians were given jobs in plantations, rural Malays were peasants, urban Malays were offered employment in the public sector, and many Chinese became entrepreneurs. Income gaps were significant. Even after independence, the Chinese continued to dominate the economic realm and this caused racial friction.

With the objective of fighting poverty among indigenous Malays, the People's Trustee Council – known by its acronym, MARA – was established in 1966. Its role was to promote indigenous entrepreneurship; it identified opportunities for Malay *bumiputras* – literally "sons of the soil" – to become entrepreneurs. Throughout the 1960s, Malaysian policy encouraged diversified, import substitution.

Following the ethnic riots of 1969, the government opted to create a policy that would achieve more economic parity between *bumiputras* and ethnic minorities. In 1970, *bumiputras* owned 2.6% of the corporate structure in Malaysia. The government's goal was for *bumiputras* to control 30.0% of the nation's capital within 20 years. (In 1999, it was still below target.)

In 1971, the New Economic Policy was launched, to fight poverty and to achieve more ethnic parity. *Bumiputras* were granted special privileges to help them purchase land, obtain business permits, and improve their economic situation.

The Second Malaysian Five-Year Plan (1971-1975) was designed to create a generation of Malay entrepreneurs. It specified that the objective of entrepreneurship training, in Malaysia, was "to foster the emergence of a full-fledged Malay entrepreneurial community, within one generation." The Ministry of Trade and Industry *Bumiputra* Participation Division was created to assist the indigenous Malays in particular, and the Export Trade Centre came to assist *bumiputras* to identify opportunities for entrepreneurship.

In 1975, the Industrial Co-ordination Act made it mandatory for all manufacturing establishments with a registered capital above 100,000 ringgits to be authorised by the Ministry of Industry. The threshold was subsequently raised to 250,000 ringgits.

The Institute Teknologi MARA (ITM), in 1975, established the Malaysian Entrepreneurship Development Centre (MEDEC), to help develop *bumiputra* entrepreneurship. The National Productivity Centre prepared a management-training package, in conjunction with MEDEC and the

National Economic Research Development Association. In 1977, MEDEC launched a three-month long, part-time, Entrepreneurship Development Programme (EDP), and in 1981 a full-time programme was introduced. The focus of the EDP was to help potential entrepreneurs, with new venture start-ups. This included a 5-day Achievement Motivation Training (AMT) component, the purpose of which was to overcome the frequent complaint that *bumiputras* suffered because of their attitude.

The Fourth Malaysian Five-Year Plan (1981-1985) provided 318 million ringgits to various agencies responsible for promoting entrepreneurship. This included the Agricultural Bank of Malaysia, and the Development Bank of Malaysia.

Also, the Central Bank of Malaysia set a maximum lending rate on loans to *bumiputras*. In addition, the Credit Guarantee Corporation introduced a credit guarantee scheme.

In 1985, small-scale entrepreneurs, in the manufacturing sector, were exempted from the requirement of applying for a manufacturing permit from the Malaysian Industrial Development Authority. To qualify for the exemption, entrepreneurs were not allowed to have more than 49 full-time employees. As well, equity was restricted to below one million ringgits.

©1999 by Leo Paul Dana
Roasting Coffee Beans at Small-Scale Processing Plant

While the Malaysia Industrial Development Berhad introduced assistance to entrepreneurs at large, the Ministry of Finance's New Investment Fund of Malaysia was created, to give priority to export-oriented projects. In addition, the state laid down specific guidelines for banks to allocate a specific proportion of their loans to small-scale entrepreneurs.

In 1986, Malaysia launched its Industrial Master Plan, emphasising the need for local firms to internationalise. In 1988, there were 28,335 manufacturers in Malaysia, of which 92.6% were small or medium industries (SMIs)[10], and four fifths of the SMIs had a capitalisation of less than 50,000 ringgits. In consideration of this bi-modal distribution of very large and very small manufacturers, the state intervened to assist SMIs. This was done with the co-operation of the Malaysian External Trade Development Corporation; the Malaysian Industrial Development Authority; the Ministry of Human Resources; the Ministry of Science, Technology and Environment; and the Prime Minister's Support Department.

The year 1990 saw the introduction of an offshore infrastructure in the Federal Territory of Labuan. This included the Offshore Banking Act, the Offshore Companies Act and the Offshore Insurance Act. As Labuan became an international, offshore financial centre, foreign entrepreneurs paid only 3% tax, or a flat fee. During the Sixth Malaysian Five-Year Plan (1991-1995), private investment in Malaysia increased by an average of 16.6% per annum.

In 1992, the Malaysian Technology Development Corporation Sdn Bhd was incorporated, as a joint venture between government and industry, to increase technology-based entrepreneurship in Malaysia. The institution operates as a venture capital company, and identifies entrepreneurs whose ventures can become high-tech companies.

In May 1996, the Seventh Malaysian Five-Year Plan (1996-2000) emphasised the importance of having an export orientation in the increasingly liberal world trade environment. Also in 1996, the Labuan Offshore Financial Services Authority was established.

Until 1998, the law required at least 30% of every company in Malaysia to be owned by *bumiputras*. To cope with this requirement, ethnic-Chinese Malaysians used *bumiputras* to register companies and to pose as majority shareholders, but without powers. Thus, *bumiputras* owned the majority of a firm (on paper), while the Chinese partners kept effective control. This was

---

[10] In Malaysia, an SMI is defined as a manufacturing company with equity not exceeding 2.5 million ringgits.

called the Ali-Baba system, Ali referring to *bumiputras* and Baba to the Chinese. In general, the Chinese disliked the *bumiputra* policy, which they described as a political instrument to limit their entrepreneurial activity. Yet, in some cases, Chinese entrepreneurs benefited by appointing influential *bumiputras* to their firms.

During the Asian Crisis, *bumiputra* entrepreneurs faced financial difficulties. The government consequently relaxed its *bumiputra* equity ownership restriction, allowing non-Malays to provide unlimited capital to some firms. Since then, ethnic-Chinese Malaysians have been allowed to own up to 100% of a local company.

Since August 1998, all new manufacturing projects have been free from equity requirements. Also, entrepreneurs who qualify for "pioneer status" have been entitled to a five-year exemption from income tax. In September 1998, Malaysia pegged its currency at a rate of 3.80 ringgits to the US dollar.

©1999 by Leo Paul Dana

Bumiputra Home

© 1999 by Leo Paul Dana

Small-Scale Enterprise in Kluang

©1999 by Leo Paul Dana

Malaysian Sugar

Toward the Future

The objective behind entrepreneurship promotion in Malaysia has been to redress economic differences between *bumiputras* and other ethnic groups in the country. Yet, Malaysian Chinese ownership of shares in local companies rose from 29% in 1969 to 41% in 1995; *bumiputra* ownership has been stable between 19% and 21% since 1990.

When the Asian Crisis affected enterprises belonging to *bumiputra* entrepreneurs, Malaysia allowed Chinese and foreign entrepreneurs to inject more capital into these ailing enterprises. In effect, such relaxation of equity restrictions allowed Chinese entrepreneurs to buy into enterprises at low, crisis-time prices. This will enable Chinese entrepreneurs to gain greater control of the economy than in the past. However, according to the Selangor Federation of Chinese Guilds and Associations, half of all entrepreneurs in Malaysia wind up their enterprise by the third year of operations.

©1999 by Leo Paul Dana

Investing in the Future

Chapter 10

The Republic of the Philippines[11]

Introduction

The Republic of the Philippines is an archipelago of over seven thousand islands, with a total land-mass of almost 300,000 square kilometres. While the national Filipino tongue is Tagalog-based, English is the language commonly used in commerce; in terms of population (approximately 70 million), the Philippines is the world's third largest English-speaking country (although not all are conversant in English).

Numerous studies have investigated entrepreneurship in the Philippines. Sharma (1979) found that entrepreneurs in the Philippines were independent and highly motivated to take risks, with a great desire to maximise their potential. The same study also asserted that the "Filipino entrepreneur is college educated and hails from a business-oriented family (p.223)." Almost a decade later, El-Namaki (1988) reported a declining level of small business self-employment in the Philippines. According to Swierczek and Jatusripatak (1994), who examined cultural features of entrepreneurship in the Philippines, entrepreneurs in this country appear to have had greater advantages than elsewhere in south-east Asia; the authors described their sample as technically skilled, innovative and opportunistic. Chen (1997) focused on small-scale retailers in the Philippines.

---

[11] The author researched this chapter in the Philippines. Courtesy transportation to the Philippines was provided on Philippine Air Lines. Methodology for this chapter included primary data collection from the Bureau of Labour and Employment; the Department of Trade & Industry; Bureau of Small and Medium Business Development; the Institute for Small Scale Industries; the Philippines Chamber of Commerce and Industry; and the Philippines Institute for Development Studies.

While the ethnic-Chinese, in the Philippines, have been very active in small business development, indigenous Filipinos have tended to exhibit a lesser incidence of entrepreneurship. Since the 1980s, several measures have been taken to broaden the appeal of enterprise and to assist Filipino entrepreneurs.

Despite efforts to promote and to finance business ventures, several constraints have hindered small enterprise development in the Philippines. This chapter gives an overview of entrepreneurship development in this archipelago.

Historical Overview

The first Westerner to discover this archipelago was Ferdinand Magellan, in 1521. The islands were already thriving with commerce, as Arab, Chinese and Indian merchants had come to trade here. King Philip II of Spain took interest in the area, and sent later expeditions; it is after him that the name Philippines was coined.

Over three centuries of Spanish rule came to an end in 1898, when independence was declared. In 1900, the United States took control, followed by the Japanese in 1942. The Americans returned during WWII, and a second republic was created in 1946.

Ferdinand Marcos acquired power in 1965 and declared martial law in 1972. He was ousted in 1986, when Corazon Aquino (widow of his assassinated opponent) took over. One of her major plans was to implement the Comprehensive Agrarian Reform Programme, which was meant to redistribute vast holdings from the elite to the rural poor; however, this programme was less successful than she had planned. Meanwhile, local entrepreneurs lobbied aggressively for an increase in protective trade barriers. Mrs. Aquino survived seven attempted coups, and a struggle with the New People's Army, the aim of which was a communist take-over. In 1992, Fidel Ramos succeeded her with a platform to create jobs, revitalise the economy, reduce foreign debt and fight corruption.

When Joseph Estrada became president, on June 30, 1998, he promised to continue market reforms. Nevertheless, as the effects of the Asian Crisis affected the economy, the jobless rate rose to its highest level in seven years. According to the Bureau of Labour and Employment, unemployment was 9.6% in October 1998. Also, the large budget deficit continued to grow.

The People

The population of the Philippines is heavily concentrated (more than 50%) on Luzon and Mindanao, the two largest islands. The indigenous Filipinos are of Malayo-Polynesian origin. The Chinese minority is an important one. About one million people in the Philippines have some Chinese ancestry and they tend to be quite visible in the realm of business. Some years ago, an article in *The Economist*[12] reported that although less than 1% of the population in the Philippines is of pure Chinese descent, firms owned by ethnic-Chinese account for two-thirds of the 67 biggest commercial outfits. The same essay added that the Chinese dominate the small business sector to an even greater degree.

Today, it is perhaps on the island of Cebu that one best sees Chinese entrepreneurship in the Philippines. Most of the entrepreneurs on this island are ethnic-Chinese and real economic growth, here, is consistently higher than is the national average.

A Tradition of Chinese Entrepreneurship

Although Spain was very successful in its efforts to convert the Filipinos to Christianity, it failed in its attempt to displace the economic prominence of Chinese entrepreneurs in the Philippines. The Spanish restricted the Chinese and often threatened violence. Between 1603 and 1762, there were constant massacres of Chinese people in the Philippines. Nevertheless, Chinese entrepreneurs continued to thrive in commerce and they mastered the Spanish language. A new class emerged – multilingual Chinese entrepreneurs.

Descendants of marriages between Christianised Chinese men and indigenous Filipinas resulted in Christian Chinese-mestizos. Both the Spanish Church and the authorities gave greater privileges to these people than to pure (non-Christian) Chinese. As a class, the Christian Chinese-mestizos were considered higher than the Chinese. Their descendants are quite different than the Peranakans in Malaysia, in the sense that the Chinese-mestizos identify themselves as Christians rather than Chinese.

---

12 "The Overseas Chinese," July 18, 1992, p.21.

During the 1700s, the largest land holdings in the Philippines were those of Christian religious orders. Wealthy Chinese entrepreneurs subsequently purchased estates from the clergy, and time widened the gap between the per capita income of economic elites and that of the masses. A priority of wealthy Chinese parents was to provide their young with educational opportunities beyond those available to the masses. The emerging educated class of elites acquired the name *ilustrados*, Spanish for "those who are enlightened."

The nineteenth century brought a new wave of immigrants from China's Fujian province. These also prospered in commerce, and in money-lending as well as agriculture. However, they had a lower social standing than the more educated, established Chinese.

Today, the ethnic-Chinese in the Philippines comprise 2% of the population; yet, they control more than half of market capitalisation. Most of them (85%) are Hokkien.

Facilitating Entrepreneurship in the Philippines

Considerable effort has focused on broadening the appeal of entrepreneurship, and entrepreneurs in the Philippines have long been assisted by foreign donors as well as by local sources.

In 1974, the Canadian International Development Agency (CIDA) sponsored the Cagayon Valley Co-operative Development Programme, to develop farmers' co-operatives in the Philippines. In 1978, the same agency launched the Industrial Co-operation Programme (ICP) which soon became involved in matching Filipino entrepreneurs with counterparts overseas. In 1981, another CIDA project was designed to assist small-scale Filipino fishermen. Additional Canadian funds were allocated to help micro-enterprises and small business development. During the late 1980s, CIDA planned an Enterprise Development Project to promote increased entrepreneurial capability in the Philippines. Support was geared to cottage industries as well as to micro-enterprises and small businesses.

The Philippine Development Assistance Programme (PDAP) is yet another project of CIDA. This project was funded by the National Initiatives Programme (of the federal government of Canada) but implemented by a non-governmental organisation. In order to maximise the input of the PDAP fund, small-scale projects were given priority, with the aim of helping self-employed tenant farmers, and fishermen among others. The initial success of the initiative led to its later enlargement.

The international organisation, Approtech Asia – based in the Philippines and financially supported by CIDA – undertook projects to help women entrepreneurs in the Philippines. Likewise, Singapore-based Technonet Asia initiated a project to assist technology transfers to the Philippines.

Meanwhile, the World Bank approved several billion dollars of loans, through the International Bank for Reconstruction and Development. Some of these funds were channelled to half a million family-farms in the Philippines. Also, the Asian Development Bank and Fund approved significant loans to provide credit to micro-enterprises and cottage industries.

Another important player, in the small business sector of the Philippines, is the International Fund for Agriculture Development, which channels aid to small-scale farmers. One of its technical assistance grants, to the International Rice Research Institute (in Los Banos, Philippines), led to research about a training programme to encourage the cultivation of azolla, which is a low-cost, natural fertiliser. Because azolla is labour-intensive (as opposed to capital-intensive), it is ideal for small-scale farmers.

Foreign aid has also contributed to the significant improvement of the telecommunication infrastructure, especially since the 1980s, when most communities in the Philippines had inadequate access to telecommunications. The situation improved during the 1990s, when the Department of Transportation and Communication received technical assistance and training from the Philippines Telecommunications Technical Assistance Project, funded by CIDA. The same Canadian agency also sponsored a project to provide a public toll call facility in each of several communities. Today, most communications services belong to the private sector.

The Philippines traditionally practised an import-substitution policy supported by high customs duties. As a result of high duties, only 20% of components in the local garment industry were sourced in the domestic market; this was true until the early 1990s. Foreign exchange controls were lifted in 1992, and the tariff structure was subsequently reformed.

The government also planned several incentives to enhance entrepreneurial spirit. Among these are industrial estates (see Table 10.1), export processing zones (in Baguio City, Bataan, Cavite, and Mactan) and special development programmes (see Table 10.2). As well, the state created tax holidays and credits to lure entrepreneurs from overseas, especially those creating labour-intensive activity in the Philippines.

Batangas City: Tabangao
Bulacan: First Bulacan Industrial Estate
Cavite: First Cavite Industrial Estate Gateway Business Industrial Estate
Isabela: Leyte
Laguna Province: Carmelary Industrial Estate Laguna International Industrial Estate Laguna Technopark Light Industry and Science Industrial Estate
Tarlac: Luisita Industrial Estate

Table 10.1. Industrial Estates in the Philippines

• Calabarzon Programme • Iligan – Cayagan de Oro Programme • Panay – Negros Agro-Industrial Programme • Samar Island Special Development Programme • South Cotabato – General Santos City Area Programme

Table 10.2. Special Development Programmes in the Philippines

The Small Enterprises Research and Development Foundation of the Philippines (SERDEF) was established by the private sector to initiate, sponsor, promote, assist and conduct research, training and development of micro-enterprises, cottage industries, and small and medium sized firms in the Philippines. The foundation works with a variety of organisations, forging linkages with government agencies, industry associations and educational institutions, such as the University of the Philippines Institute for

Small Scale Industries. SERDEF has funded several publications, including: *Introduction to Entrepreneurship; Credit Manual for Small and Medium Enterprises; Filipino Women in Business: A Case Book;* and *You, Too, Can Start Your Own Business.*

The Institute for Small Scale Industries offers dozens of training courses to assist entrepreneurs. These include Financial Management; Young Entrepreneurs' Programme; Strategic Marketing; Total Quality Management; Production Management; Business Franchising; Entrepreneurial Career Development; and Appreciation Course on Entrepreneurship. The institute also offers a small business-consulting course. In addition, a trainer's course on entrepreneurship development is given. This course explains entrepreneurship strategies, and teaches participants to design, implement, monitor and evaluate entrepreneurship development programmes. An advanced course, offered by the Institute, is the Project Appraisal, Evaluation and Monitoring Course for Small and Medium Enterprise Projects. This course upgrades skills in appraising, monitoring and evaluating small and medium scale enterprise projects. A very specialised course offering is entitled Designing and Implementing Entrepreneurship Programmes for Women. This course focuses on cultural, social, legal and other barriers to female entrepreneurship and how to overcome them.

Finally, yet another player in the promotion of entrepreneurship in the Philippines is the Philippine Foundation for Resources Management. Among its projects is the Program on Women's Involvement in Entrepreneurship.

With a more limited scope is the Business Action Centre of the Naga City Chamber of Commerce, on the island of Luzon. It provides a variety of accounting and legal assistance as well as physical facilities, secretarial support, desktop publishing and courier services.

Private enterprise initiatives have also been central to the development of the transportation infrastructure. The government has allowed private firms to build toll roads and to operate them at a profit.

Given that the archipelago is spread across 1,839 kilometres, inter-island transportation relies heavily on the aeroplane. Several airlines provide domestic flights to over forty airports. Entrepreneur William Gatchalian established Air Philippines, in 1974. His friend, Lucio Tan acquired Philippine Air Lines (PAL), in 1990. Aerolift and Pacific Airways (not to be confused with Air Pacific of Fiji) provide regional services. Since the advent of the 1997 Asian crisis, however, entrepreneurs have been seeking ways to cut down on expenditures, and because air transportation is the most expensive option, some entrepreneurs have begun reconsidering using air services. Although boat links are frequent and much more affordable, this alternative is considerably slower.

© 1999 by Leo Paul Dana
Upstairs on the PAL Boeing 747: Sleeperette Service

Uncertain Future

After 57 years of service, PAL shut down on September 23, 1998. Executives cited a labour dispute as the primary cause.

Within Manila, forms of public transport include jeepneys and a Light Rail Transit (LRT) system. Taxis have been reporting less business than before the crisis.

Constraints on Entrepreneurship

As is evident from the above, many efforts have focused on financing entrepreneurs and on developing an efficient infrastructure for them. Yet, despite efforts by governmental and non-governmental bodies to foster development in the Philippines, the national economy – except Chinese-dominated Cebu – is still characterised by inflation, underdevelopment and slow growth. According to interviews conducted by the author in the Philippines, causal variables include corruption and until recently, power shortages were a problem.

Personal relationships are very important in the Filipino business sphere, and much time is spent on *pakikisama* – the development of inter-personal ties. Among the most important ties in business are those between entrepreneurs and the government, especially a practice known as *lagacy* (a polite word for "buying personal ties"). Officials expect bribes in return for allowing entrepreneurship to flourish. Some entrepreneurs have long-established channels of bribery, and these are used to create barriers to entry. This effectively inhibits potential new entrants, and limits competition. Entrepreneurs are often approached by individuals offering "protection" for small firms, in exchange for special payments, locally known as *tong*. This is effectively a bribe without which an entrepreneur's business can be put in jeopardy.

Finally, an adequate supply of affordable energy is essential for economic development, and for a healthy entrepreneurship sector. Beginning in 1983, the Petro-Canada International Assistance Corporation began a programme of co-operation with the Bureau of Energy and Development. Also, loans were extended to the Philippines National Oil Company and to the National Power Corporation. The objective was to exploit an existing geothermal steam field, construct a power station and improve power transmission lines. Yet, the nation is still dependent on imported petrol. A setback occurred during the Asian Crisis, when the national currency tumbled, raising the effective price of imports sold in US dollars.

The Entrepreneurship Sector Today

The economy of the Philippines is a blend of agriculture, fishing and light industry; small enterprises are major players. On family farms, important crops include *abaca* (a fibre related to the banana plant), bananas, coconuts, coffee, copra, corn, hemp, nuts, pineapples, rice, sugarcane, tapioca, tobacco, vegetables and yams. Both subsistence farming and subsistence fishing are common to this day.

Although the nation could have been self-sufficient in food, it is not. The low yields can be traced to a tradition of absentee landlords in a peasant society.

Clothing and food-processing are the most developed industries, along with the light manufacturing of home appliances. Sectors showing growth include aquaculture, furniture assembly and microcircuit production. Most exports are manufactured goods such as electrical microcircuits and semi-conductors.

Some literature (Halloran 1991; Kinyanjui, 1993) has suggested that for some countries the growth of the entrepreneurship sector is constrained by the lack of easy access to financing. This is *not* the case in the Philippines. During the early 20th century, missionaries introduced to these islands the concept of co-operatives. Basing these co-operatives on the rural credit unions of the United States, the missionaries launched a movement that eventually gained considerable popularity. Today, several hundred credit unions provide low-cost capital to entrepreneurs who lack collateral. Chinese entrepreneurs have their own credit circles. In addition, foreign entrepreneurs provide financing to informal enterprises sometimes without collateral.

Toward the Future

It has been shown that entrepreneurs in the Philippines have a great deal going for them. Several programmes were created to help small enterprises and cottage industries. Entrepreneurship is even fostered at the Iwahig Penal Colony (on Palawan Island), where prisoners are forced to make and sell handicrafts.

The government has lifted exchange controls and reformed the tariff structure. In May 1998, the central bank reduced the reserve requirement for banks, from 10% to 8%. This led to the lowering of the prime lending rate. By June, one could obtain a loan for 16% (compared to 30%, six months earlier).

Unlike the situation described in other countries, neither financing nor infrastructure is problematic here. In the case of the Philippines, entrepreneurship is limited mostly by corruption and by the insufficient access to affordable energy. Affected by the Asian Crisis, growth slowed down; the IMF forecasted 3.8% growth for 1998. Unemployment rose and inflation was projected to rise too.

Chapter 11

The Republic of Singapore[13]

Introduction

At the tip of peninsular Malaysia lies Singapore, a city-republic covering one main island (23 kilometres from north to south and 42 kilometres wide), and some tiny islets, the latter mostly uninhabited. Its area is 646 square kilometres, and it is home to almost 100,000 small and medium-size enterprises.

Since its early years, the Singapore Government created a positive investment climate, attracting multinational corporations to a free port with a business-friendly environment. Foreign firms responded; they brought their technologies, created employment, and contributed to economic development. As foreign firms began to shift operations to lower-cost locations, the Singapore Government began encouraging its own entrepreneurs to thrive. However, market saturation in Singapore soon threatened the survival of many local entrepreneurs; internationalisation of entrepreneurship became a necessity.

---

[13] The author researched this chapter in Singapore, bringing together information collected from a variety of agencies, including: the Construction Industry Development Board; the Economic Development Board; the Enterprise Promotion Centres Pte Ltd; the National Science & Technology Board; the Singapore Productivity and Standards Board; the Singapore Tourism Board; and the Trade Development Board. The author is also grateful to Deputy Prime Minister Dr. Tony Tan Keng Yan, and to Professor Tommy Koh for personally sharing some thoughts.

Historical Overview

Pre-Colonial Times

A Chinese document from the third century referred to Singapore as *Pu Luo Chung*, literally meaning, "island at the tip of a peninsula." Because of its location, at the tip of a peninsula between China and India, traders already knew this island.

While Marco Polo referred to Singapore as *Malayur* (Tamil for "Hill Town"), the Javanese called it *Temasek*, meaning "Sea Town." The harbour made it attractive to Arab, Chinese, and Indian merchants, who came to trade with entrepreneurs from Java, Malaya and Siam (as Thailand was then known). The Sumatra-based Srivijaya Empire ruled the region, including the Malayan Peninsula and the islands of Java and Sumatra.

In 1299, on the island of *Temasek*, a prince from Sumatra saw an animal that he could not identify. An elder said it might be a lion. It was probably a tiger, as lions have never been indigenous to this area. Nevertheless, the island came to be known as *Singapura*, meaning "Lion City" in Sanskrit. Later, the name was anglicised to its present form, Singapore.

Merchants from Arab lands, and others from India, frequently passed by Singapore. These entrepreneurs were the middlemen in the spice trade between Indonesia and Europe. During the early 1500s, Europeans began coming to this part of the world, to obtain spices directly. In the sub-continent, the British established the British East India Company. An increase in demand for Chinese tea, silk and pottery, among European consumers, prompted the company to send expeditions from India to China.

Sir Thomas Stamford Raffles

In 1781, Thomas Stamford Raffles was born at sea, into a poor family living in London. At the time, the British were interested in India for its tea, and their trading arm was the British East India Company. The firm had trading posts in Bombay, Calcutta and Madras (today's Chennai). From India, the company sent ships to China, to obtain pottery and silk. Since the journey between India and China was a lengthy one, it was therefore decided to set up a node along the way, where British ships could stop for water, food and repairs. Accordingly, in 1786, the British East India Company set up a base in Penang.

In 1795, 14-year-old Thomas began working for the British East India Company, in London. Ten years later, the company sent him to Penang, where he learned Malay. In 1811, he was put in charge of Java, where he abolished slavery. In 1818, he was transferred to Bencoolen, a British trading post on the island of Sumatra. This was before Sumatra became Dutch.

In 1819, Sir Thomas Stamford Raffles, Lieutenant-Governor of Bencoolen, selected Singapore as the location for a new port for the British East India Company. Raffles paid the local leaders for permission to set up a free port, and this attracted thousands of entrepreneurs. Raffles segregated different ethnic groups into assigned neighbourhoods.

When the British took full control of Singapore, in 1824, the settlement had 10,683 people, of whom 31% were Chinese. In 1826, Singapore became part of the British Straits Settlements, along with Malacca and Penang. That year, a famine in China prompted 4,000 men to come to Singapore. When Chinese men had children with Malay women, the offspring were known as Baba Chinese or Straits Chinese. Their descendants are known as Peranakans.

©1999 by Leo Paul Dana

The Chinese Brought Mandarin Script and Chinese Medicine to Singapore

©1999 by Leo Paul Dana

Entrepot Trade: Bank of China Warehouse on Robertson Quay

A Centre of Entrepreneurship

In 1867, the Straits Settlements became a Crown Colony. The inauguration of the Suez Canal, in 1869, made Singapore an important node along the route from England to Australia. This helped the growth of Singapore as a centre of international trade. Entrepreneurs set up go-downs (warehouses) and trading houses. Singapore became a centre for entrepot trade.

The British were interested in the development of modern capitalism in Singapore. They promoted trade and commerce, in an environment of minimal regulation. This attracted entrepreneurs from countries such as Burma, Iraq, Syria, and of course China.

Many migrants from China were sojourners who intended to eventually return to their homeland. Since these people had no long-term commitment to the British colony, they usually avoided capital-intensive industries, which required long pay-back periods. Thus, the ethnic-Chinese in Singapore were largely concentrated in commerce, an activity in which gains were more immediate. Gasse (1982) cited the pre-war Chinese community in Singapore as cultivating entrepreneurs more easily than others. It should be noted, however, that these entrepreneurs were mostly merchants, not industrialists.

On February 15, 1942, the Japanese took control of Singapore, renaming it *Syonan-to*, Japanese for "Light of the South." Although the British returned after the Japanese surrender, an independence movement began to grow.

The year 1946 saw the break-up of the Straits Settlements, as Malacca and Penang joined the Malayan Union. In 1959, Singapore obtained self-government. In 1963, it joined Malaya, Sabah and Sarawak to form Malaysia and on August 9, 1965, Singapore became an independent republic. Until 1985, Singapore relied on foreign multinational corporations to industrialise the nation and to develop the economy. At the time, there was no perceived need to encourage local entrepreneurs. However, a global recession that year led the government to realise the vulnerability of a domestic economy which relied very heavily on foreign capital and overseas markets. At that time, focus shifted to entrepreneurship and more recently to technopreneurship, as Singapore rushed to become a regional technology hub.

©1999 by Leo Paul Dana

Selling Durians in Chinatown

A Multicultural Society

Singapore was built by people of numerous cultural backgrounds, including Malays, Tamils, and ethnic-Chinese from different provinces of China. From Fujian province came Foochows (speaking Fuzhouhua), Henghuas (speaking Xinghuahua), Hokchias (speaking Fuquinhua) and Hokkiens (speaking Minnanhua). Cantonese people (speaking Guangzhouhua), and Teochews (speaking Chaozhouhua) came from Guang Dong. Hainanese immigrants (speaking Hainanhua) came from Hainan Island. Hakkas (speaking Kehua) came from Fujian and Guang Dong. The Hokkiens are the largest ethno-cultural group in Singapore.

©1999 by Leo Paul Dana
Scripts in Singapore: Chinese, Arabic & Latin

For linguistic reasons, people tended to live among, and to work with others, who spoke the same dialect. When new immigrants arrived, they worked for entrepreneurs. This led to considerable occupational clustering. The Hokkiens – who had political contacts with the colonial government – became very involved in entrepot trade. Many traded along Chulia Street. Other Hokkien entrepreneurs lived on China Street, where they sold sundry items as well as fresh greens. Telok Ayer Street was home to larger-scale Hokkien entrepreneurs who imported goods from neighbouring countries.

The Teochews dominated the rice trade across south-east Asia. In Singapore, Teochews could be found along Circular Road, not far from the Singapore River. On Chin Chew Street, they traded spices. On Chulia Street, Teochew dealers sold bird's nest and shark's fin.

Under the leadership of Mr. Aw Boon Haw, producer of Tiger Balm, Hakka entrepreneurs dominated Singapore's medicine halls. The Cantonese were regarded as a lower class. They were clustered in the district around Kreta Ayer. Many sold cloth. Some sold furniture, musical instruments, tobacco and silk, which they imported from China. They had shop-houses on Pagoda Street and on Temple Street. Others were artisans, goldsmiths, tailors and restaurant-owners.

©1999 by Leo Paul Dana

A Famous Restaurant Used to be the Colonial, in the Ellison Building

To foster co-operation among people sharing the same dialect, and to promote commercial and industrial development, entrepreneurs established and joined clan associations. Mingling with other members helped individuals understand trends in product development as well as price fluctuations. Here, entrepreneurs could discuss partnerships and obtain financing. Clan associations provided social contacts, training, business ideas, market information, business concepts, start-up capital and technical assistance. This web of networking played an important role in the development of entrepreneurship in Singapore.

The Hokkien Hui Kuan (Hokkien Clan Association) donated land to build Nanyang University, which opened in 1958. This was the first Chinese-language university outside China. After independence, nationalism transcended clan loyalties, and clan associations lost their dominance.

©1999 by Leo Paul Dana

Nanyang University

Singapore society, today, is quite heterogeneous. Buddhists comprise 28% of the population, while 19% are Christian, 16% are Muslim, 13% are Tao and 5% are Hindu.

The behaviours and values of the Chinese in Singapore are deep-rooted in Confucian dynamism, which includes the virtues of perseverance and thrift. Both of these factors tend to facilitate entrepreneurship. Singaporeans have been discouraged from believing in extreme individualism. Instead, they have been conditioned to feel a loyalty to the nuclear and extended family. They accept that the family is the building block of society. Divorce rates are low. All these factors may be said to have contributed to the success of family business in Singapore.

Singaporeans are also taught the importance of saving, frugality and hard work. These factors, when coupled with compulsory Central Providence Fund (CPF) contributions, have made Singapore's savings equal to 46% of GNP – the highest in the world. When entrepreneurs need capital for new ventures or to expand existing firms, informal financing is often available.

Confucian values have served as guidelines for social norms, which may help entrepreneurship. However, research has not found ethnic-Chinese cultural values to emphasise initiative. Although the Singapore Government once relied on foreign investors for economic growth, since 1985 there has been emphasis on encouraging Singaporeans to develop initiatives in the realm of entrepreneurship.

Public Policy on Entrepreneurship in Singapore

In 1985, BG Lee Hsien Loong, the Acting Minister of Trade and Industry and Chairman of the Committee on Small Enterprise Policy, stated: "We must have our own entrepreneurs... We need a focal point for small business, a single agency to co-ordinate these schemes, work out new ones, and provide one-stop service for small enterprises." He was introducing the Small Enterprise Bureau of Singapore, with programmes to help entrepreneurs. The Singapore Government allocated S$100 million to this end, and the Small Enterprise Bureau was established as a division of the Singapore Development Board, for the purpose of helping promising entrepreneurs.

Until 1995, the Economic Development Board was in charge of small and medium-size enterprise development. Its Small and Medium Enterprise

(SME) Master Plan emphasised local entrepreneurship. That year, the Singapore Productivity and Standards Board was created. The new agency's mission was to raise productivity such as to enhance Singapore's competitiveness and economic growth for a better quality of life. It also took the responsibility to promote entrepreneurship in Singapore.

The Singapore Productivity and Standards Board developed a three-pronged strategy to promote entrepreneurship:

- broad-based assistance to small and medium size firms;
- focused assistance to selected, promising entrepreneurs; and
- industry-wide assistance.

During 1996 – its first year of operations – the Singapore Productivity and Standards Board provided broad-based assistance to more than 2,500 small and medium enterprises. This assistance was implemented through its Local Enterprise Upgrading Centre.

The Singapore Productivity and Standards Board helps entrepreneurs participate in a variety of Government Development Assistance Programmes. Under the industry-wide assistance scheme, the Singapore Productivity and Standards Board facilitates the creation of new franchises. The Board also helps entrepreneurs to harness information technology. For instance, Shopnet links small-scale retailers with suppliers, and financial assistance is offered to entrepreneurs who wish to adopt the system. Funding comes from the Local Enterprise Technical Assistance Scheme. Additional money to train entrepreneurs how to use Shopnet is available from the Skills Development Fund.

Various agencies are responsible for the different government assistance programmes. For example, there are two capital loan programmes. The Singapore Productivity and Standards Board administers the Local Enterprise Finance Scheme, while the Economic Development Board helps entrepreneurs expand beyond local markets.

There are also business development grants. The Trade Development Board administers grants to assist entrepreneurs in developing their brand names. The Economic Development Board has a Local Industry Upgrading Programme to foster ties between multinational corporations and smaller-scale suppliers of parts and services in Singapore. The Singapore Productivity and Standards Board assists companies to engage professional expertise to oversee the implementation of strategic plans for expansion.

©1999 by Leo Paul Dana

The David Elias Buildings

©1999 by Leo Paul Dana

Shophouses on Middle Road

©1999 by Leo Paul Dana

Storefronts on Selegie Road

©1999 by Leo Paul Dana

The Corner of North Bridge Road and Middle Road

Other programmes, administered by the Singapore Productivity and Standards Board, include the Partners-in-Training Scheme, the Research and Development Incubator Programme, and the SME Manager Scheme. The first of these encourages wholesalers and franchisers to train their small and medium-sized enterprise partners, such as retailers and franchisees, for mutual gain. The Research and Development Incubator Programme facilitates research and development by Singaporean entrepreneurs, by offering laboratory space in the Science Park.

In addition, there are business innovation grants such as the Innovator's Assistance Scheme, administered by the National Science and Technology Board. The objective of this programme is to assist innovators and investors to develop their concepts into commercially viable processes and products.

As well, there are Information Technology Application Grants. For instance, the Innovation Development scheme encourages and assists entrepreneurs to engage in the innovation of processes, products, applications and services. The Local Entreprise Accounting Programme introduces and implements systematic and effective financial reporting and management systems to small and medium enterprises. In 1999, the Supreme Court unveiled a new scheme, offering contractual manufacturers a waiver of GST.

This section has illustrated that various loans, grants and tax incentives are available for entrepreneurs in Singapore. The wide range of programmes covers financing, business development, management, productivity improvement, manpower training, marketing, exporting, technology transfer, information technology and automation. Some programmes are for new venture start-ups, and others for expansion or internationalisation. The next section shall address government attempts to internationalise entrepreneurship from Singapore.

Internationalising Singaporean Entrepreneurs

In the late 1980s, the Singapore Government began promoting the "Growth Triangle," giving incentives for Singaporean entrepreneurs to relocate manufacturing activities to Indonesia and Malaysia. However, internationalisation was limited.

It was in 1993 that Senior Minister Lee Kuan Yew declared, "We can enthuse a younger generation with the thrill and the rewards of building an external dimension to Singapore. We can and we will spread our wings into the region and then into the wider world."

Notwithstanding Singapore's attractiveness to foreign multinational corporations, Singaporean entrepreneurs can also play a role in international business. Given the limited size of Singapore's domestic market, internationalisation would help Singaporean entrepreneurs to achieve economies of scale. Thus, internationalisation can improve local production.

Hence, the Singapore Government has been promoting the internationalisation of Singaporean entrepreneurship. Among the incentives are a variety of Going Regional Grants, some of which are administered by the Economic Development Board. Examples include the Malaysia-Singapore Third Country Investment Feasibility Study Fund. The purpose of this programme is to encourage Singaporean firms to undertake, jointly with their Malaysian counterparts, feasibility studies on pursuing joint investment and business projects in third countries. Another programme administered by the Economic Development Board is the Singapore-Australia Business Alliance Forum Joint Feasibility Study Fund. This programme encourages Singaporean entrepreneurs to set up joint ventures with Australians, again in third countries. The Economic Development Board also has a Business Development Scheme, which assists Singaporean entrepreneurs to identify opportunities abroad. The Trade Development Board has a Franchise Development Assistance Scheme, the purpose of which is to encourage Singaporean entrepreneurs to develop a franchise package and to market the concept overseas.

The Association of Small and Medium Enterprises has also been promoting the internationalisation of Singaporean small and medium enterprises. In 1998, it launched SME Day, with networking events for entrepreneurs, under the theme Towards Globalisation.

In September 1998, the first conference on international entrepreneurship brought together leading academics from around the world. It was decided that Singapore's Nanyang Technological University would sponsor the second conference, at the Goodwood Park Hotel, in Singapore, August 15-18, 1999. As the domestic market in Singapore became increasingly saturated, it became increasingly important for Singaporean entrepreneurs to look beyond Singapore.

©1999 by Leo Paul Dana

The Straits Clinic

Technopreneurship 21

During a parliamentary debate, in November 1998, it was announced to have a special committee to promote technology-based entrepreneurship, in Singapore. Deputy Prime Minister Dr. Tony Tan saw the Asian Crisis as an opportunity to accelerate the transition of the island republic to a knowledge-based economy, and a high-powered panel was organised to create a climate conducive to boosting high-tech entrepreneurship. Technological entrepreneurship was termed "technopreneurship" and ingredients were identified to promote it. These included: the availability of creative talent (foreign and local); low barriers to entry; easy access to capital; easy access to markets; tolerance of failure; and high gains. Dr. Tony Tan, chairman of the Technopreneurship 21 Ministerial Committee, explained, "Technopreneurs serve as the critical interface between ideas and markets, translating creative ideas into vehicles to serve market demand."

Toward the Future

Prior to independence, entrepreneurs in Singapore thrived as merchants. The colony was an important hub of entrepot trade, but it had few industrialists. During the 1950s, the Khong Guan Biscuit Factory produced biscuits in Indonesia. Similarly, Ho Rih Hua opened a manufacturing plant in Thailand. However, such examples were exceptions. Singapore's entrepreneurship sector was lacking in industrialists, and was limited by a distinctly local orientation. Singaporean entrepreneurs had few foreign direct investments.

After independence, the government designed an enterprise-friendly environment to attract foreign direct investment from abroad. Multinational corporations were handed the task of industrialising Singapore. More recently, the state has been encouraging both entrepreneurship and the internationalisation of entrepreneurs.

Singapore, at the turn of the millennium, has two types of entrepreneurs. One set is comprised of elder individuals who became entrepreneurs because they lacked formal education and could not compete in educated Singapore. These people were motivated by money. Failure would bring shame to their families, and so they worked very diligently to succeed. They attribute their success to hard work, patience, persistence and luck. Although successful in their home market, they tend not to venture abroad.

In contrast, the other set of entrepreneurs consists of young, educated individuals. Power and fulfilment motivate them in addition to money. Most importantly, they are expansion-oriented. Yet, they are not many in number.

In the future, according to Senior Minister Lee, "How well we do depends on how many entrepreneurs or wealth creators we have in our midst."[14] However, given the high salaries provided by multinational corporations, many Singaporeans identify a huge opportunity cost with becoming entrepreneurs. Unlike the poor Chinese migrants who lacked alternatives in colonial Singapore, non-enterprising Singaporeans can become very successful in corporate life, without becoming entrepreneurs.

©1997 by Leo Paul Dana

The Ah Chew Hotel

---

[14] Source: *The Straits Times*, July 11, 1996.

Old & New

Chapter 12

Entrepreneurship in Taiwan[15]

Introduction

Taiwan is an island with an area of 35,751 square kilometres, off the coast of China. Here, credit policy has traditionally been tight. Loans have been expensive and difficult to secure. Consequently, most firms in Taiwan are small, and tightly held. Entrepreneurs typically exert an over-riding influence on their enterprises. Even large companies tend to be owned by families, with a senior family member being the central decision-maker. Lin (1998) reported that of 935,000 entrepreneurs in Taiwan, 96.5% are small or medium enterprises, collectively employing 78.6% of the workforce. Taiwan has more entrepreneurs per capita than does any other nation in south-east Asia.

Each country has its mix of large businesses and smaller firms. The ratio depends on a variety of factors. Environmental forces, such as a government's credit policy, may greatly influence the ratio and relative importance of small enterprises to large ones. This chapter discusses entrepreneurship in Taiwan, in the context of the national credit policy.

---

[15] The author researched this chapter in Taiwan. The contents rely heavily on interviews conducted with entrepreneurs, as well as information provided from: the Board of Foreign Trade; the Directorate-General, Accounting & Statistics; and the Ministry of Economic Affairs. It is not easy to obtain financial data from Taiwanese entrepreneurs, as tax evasion is very widely practised here. In fact, many firms typically have two sets of books and entrepreneurs often have two sets of stories.

Historical Overview

The island today known as Taiwan was settled during the fourteenth century, by Han Chinese from southern China. The Portuguese arrived in 1517, and named it *Ilha Formosa*, literally the island of beauty.

In 1624, the island was claimed by the Dutch East India Company. Under Dutch rule, the island became a trans-shipping hub for international commerce. Its economic importance increased Chinese interest in the island, and by 1662 the Dutch were defeated and Formosa became Chinese.

In 1858, the Chinese allowed the British and the French to establish trading facilities on the island. Eventually, the French occupied a piece of Formosa, but in 1895 the Japanese claimed the entire island as theirs.

For fifty years, Japan ruled Formosa as a colony. Fiscal incentives encouraged the establishment of firms which were owned by Japanese entrepreneurs and which in turn, produced for the Japanese market.

At the end of World War II, Formosa was returned to China. When the communists took-over China, Chiang Kai-shek and almost two million followers fled to Taiwan. In 1950, Chiang Kai-shek became president of Taiwan.

When Taiwan was established as its own country, it was largely agricultural, and manufacturing was limited to light industries, such as sugar refining and the production of fibres. The state nationalised assets that had been controlled by the Japanese, and the government set out to develop a comprehensive economic policy suitable for the nation's situation.

Taiwan's first national policy was known as the Four Year Economic Construction Plan. At the time, it seemed reasonable to produce for the national market. Thus, in 1953, Taiwan adopted a policy of import substitution. This boosted local, small-scale enterprise. However, the size of the Taiwanese market limited local growth. Therefore, in 1958, the government adopted a new policy of export promotion.

Taiwanese entrepreneurs began to produce electric machinery for export. To facilitate export-development, a free access zone was established in Kaohsiung. The government also developed export-processing zones in Nantze and in Taichung. The purpose of these zones was to encourage industrial development, to facilitate technology transfer, and to promote exports. This new policy proved very successful, and the zones still offer several incentives, such as exemptions from duties and taxes. The high success rate of industrial parks led to the establishment of another 87, some of which are owned by entrepreneurs.

During the 1980s, the Taiwanese economy shifted to a service orientation. Beginning in 1987, entrepreneurs in Taiwan realised that their small businesses could not survive by simply undertaking local labour-intensive production. This prompted the internationalisation of Taiwanese entrepreneurs to its ASEAN neighbours.

By 1996, Taiwanese firms had 241 projects in Vietnam, representing $3.6 billion US. This was a larger investment in Vietnam than any other single country made.

Taiwanese entrepreneurs have also been active in China. The average Taiwanese investment in China is $800,000. Indeed, Taiwanese entrepreneurs have been contributing significantly to the economic development of Pacific Asia.

© 1999 by Leo Paul Dana

Contributing to Economic Development

The Impact of Credit Policy on Entrepreneurship in Taiwan

Two models can be used to describe the credit policy framework of nations:

Model I

In consideration of the fact that high interest rates may cause a heavy debt burden on entrepreneurs, while decreasing the rate of new venture formation and increasing the rate of bankruptcies, the government intervenes with subsidised interest rates, helping a few favoured borrowers. Subsidised interest rates, below the market-clearing rate, help few privileged entrepreneurs, while creating jobs for the masses. This is the model which was adopted by South Korea, and which led to the growth of the *chaebols*, very diversified and powerful mega-conglomerates.

©1999 by Leo Paul Dana

Snakes at a Market in Taiwan

Model II

Subsidised rates are considered unjust, as low-cost money encourages capital intensive methods of production, consequently limiting employment growth. Therefore, interest rates rise with market demand. High real interest rates encourage savings and keep inflation under control by reducing demand. The formal financial systems have rigid financing regulations. This is the model adopted by Taiwan.

The Case of Taiwan

Since 1950, the economy of Taiwan has followed the path of Model II, letting its interest rates rise to high market levels. This policy resulted in the world's highest rates of savings, and efficient investment in atomised industrial structures. Savings per capita, in Taiwan, have been traditionally high.

Taiwan bloomed largely because of the efforts of small-scale entrepreneurs, with thousands of entrepreneurial small businesses. Due to high interest rates, each firm had minimal debt. *The Economist* of July 14, 1990 estimated that 80% of the firms in Taiwan had fewer than twenty employees (p. 20).

A consequence of a Model II type policy, the typical firm in Taiwan is small and equity-based. The selection of such an approach has allowed policy to remain stable with no major corrections necessary along the path to prosperity. Entrepreneurs often boast that their firms have no debt.

Taiwan's experience with a Model II approach gave rise to a multitude of successful small businesses thriving in a healthy economy. The lack of larger firms does have its drawbacks, however, as research and development is fragmented among many tiny companies causing energy to be expended in duplication of efforts. As a solution for this problem, the government set up co-operative research institutes such as the Industrial Technology Research Institute.

Another shortcoming which may be attributed to a Model II approach is that small firms may lack economies of scale. However, Taiwan's low overheads, good infrastructure, and excellent network of local suppliers all help compensate for any disadvantage due to size. Local suppliers being small, a firm may be required to deal with several of them. This reduces risks, as compared to dealing with only one supplier overseas.

Perhaps the most serious problem arising from a Model II approach is that the multitude of small firms often lacks marketing expertise. Yet, a solution to this has been found – linking up with firms abroad, with marketing expertise specific to foreign markets.

Today, small industries are the backbone of Taiwan, and these small industries have become internationally competitive; 300 have become large, without government assistance. Yet, unlike the Koreans, the Taiwanese decided that global brand creation was inappropriately costly for a capital-scarce nation.

Whereas South Korea's implementation of Model I has necessitated many corrections, Taiwan's success with Model II has necessitated fewer corrections. Other countries might learn from the experience of these two tigers and their contrasting styles. In both cases, a healthy small business sector comes into existence, sooner (as in Taiwan) or later (as in South Korea after corrections). However, the Asian Crisis has shown that Model II is more sustainable. In contrast to the situation arising in states where subsidised credit is available, entrepreneurs in Taiwan borrow principally from the informal market, and at higher rates. This encourages them to focus on labour-intensive activities while optimising the use of capital.

Taiwanese Entrepreneurs & the Asian Crisis

Entrepreneurs in Taiwan tend to combine management and ownership into one function. They like to have power over their firms, and they often prefer a sole proprietorship to other forms of enterprise. They also have a higher self-funded proportion of capital than do large-scale enterprises.

As a consequence of a Model II type policy in Taiwan, Taiwanese entrepreneurs have relied relatively little on loans. Consequently, they have coped with the Asian Crisis better than have their neighbouring counterparts. By limiting external sources of income, Taiwanese entrepreneurs have reduced their risks. On the other hand, limited capital has also limited their opportunities for economies of scale.

To compensate for the lack of scale, economies of scope have been emerging. Entrepreneurs in Taiwan are willing to produce a large variety of similar products, albeit in relatively small quantities. For example, the process of production is similar for steel car-plates and machinery-shells.

Therefore, one firm can easily make both items. Nevertheless, entrepreneurs usually do so only after receiving specific orders.

In contrast to large corporations, which have heavy capital investments, entrepreneurs in Taiwan have relatively less fixed production equipment. This makes it easy to adapt facilities in order to modify products or to produce different items, as necessary. This allows Taiwanese entrepreneurs to adapt rapidly to changing needs.

Entrepreneurs in Taiwan also respond quickly to changes in purchasing power. Owner-managers are often involved in sales as well as in production. They know their costs, and can rapidly adjust prices according to market demand. This ability is very helpful during crises.

Large-scale enterprises, which tend to be more formal in their organisational structure, have depth and breadth. In contrast, entrepreneurs in Taiwan tend to have few employees outside family members and friends. Furthermore, in a traditional Taiwanese firm, the founder is generally the role model for employees. These factors allow entrepreneurs to lean toward emotion for the smooth operation of their firms. Emphasis is on team-work.

The situation in Taiwan is such that manufacturing processes are flexibly organised among entrepreneurs, each optimising on efficiency brought about by the division of labour among firms. Although the division of work among firms is clear, the division of labour within a small firm is vague. Employees are often asked to do more than required by their respective job descriptions, and they usually comply. This includes personal sacrifice, when the entrepreneurs need extra input. In turn, this reduces costs and contributes to the profitability of entrepreneurship in Taiwan. During the crisis, employees have been asked to make due with less.

As discussed by Lin (1998), successful entrepreneurs in Taiwan focus on people-related issues rather than structure or technology, and there is more concern with attitudes and skills than with equipment. Entrepreneurs, here, do not perceive a need to be the vanguard of technological innovation. As long as there is a demand for existing goods, made with existing technology, entrepreneurs are not in a rush to change production methods.

It seems that this focus on people was instrumental in helping Taiwan move away from the crisis. A Chinese saying suggests that plants, scorched by flames, surge back with the spring wind. So too, it appears that the entrepreneurs of Taiwan will surge back.

Toward the Future

Limited by capital, entrepreneurs in Taiwan seldom produce a product from scratch. Most have prospered as suppliers of parts. Many have concentrated on the manufacturing of consigned components; in these cases, marketing has not been very important, because an entrepreneur needed few clients.

In other contexts, when enterprises grow, entrepreneurs often wish to become involved in producing goods from start to finish. In Taiwan, however, growth-oriented entrepreneurs often expect to encounter difficulties. Banks are reluctant to lend capital to entrepreneurs in Taiwan, especially considering that many enterprises lack a sound accounting system. Bankers reported to the author that financial reports are often incorrect.

Nevertheless, although small — by world standards — Taiwanese firms serve their purpose. Neither government nor financing is central to entrepreneurship in here. Nor are technological innovations perceived as important. The focus is on people. The establishment of a new venture creates jobs for the entrepreneur's family, and sometimes for strangers who become adopted as family members of the firm. The small size of most firms facilitates communications. A friendly, teacher-apprentice relationship is superimposed on the entrepreneur-employee relation. As job descriptions are vague, employees fill in for one another. People develop a width of professional knowledge, but often lack depth. The work environment is friendly. Yet, non-family members have few opportunities for promotion. Therefore, turnover is high.

Entrepreneurs, in Taiwan, rely very much on personal networks, for market information, for suppliers, for clients and for employees. This approach combines the economic and social activities of entrepreneurs. One very important economic and social activity is gift-giving. Gifts are very symbolic in Taiwan, and neglecting an opportunity for gift-giving may be perceived as poor conduct. Similarly, an inappropriate gift (such as clocks, knives, handkerchiefs, scissors and watches) may sever relations. Gifts to tax collectors are especially wise investments.

> *Those who gain the hearts of the people prosper;*
> *Those who disappoint the people, perish.*
>
> – Chinese proverb

Pork is Eaten Frequently in Taiwan

Chapter 13

The Kingdom of Thailand[16]

Introduction

Neighbouring Cambodia, Laos, Myanmar and Malaysia, the Kingdom of
Thailand covers 514,000 square kilometres. An independent, sovereign state
for over seven centuries, Thailand is the only country in south-east Asia that
has never been colonised. During the latter half of the twentieth century, the
nation's industrial structure was transformed from that of a primary product
producer to a major manufacturer. Under the Ministry of Commerce, the
Department of Export Promotion was established to promote Thai exports
overseas. In 1984, devaluation helped boost Thai exports. Textile exports
have since surpassed rice exports. In 1997, however, the fall of the baht
initiated the Asian Crisis.

---

[16] The author researched this chapter in Thailand. Transportation to Thailand was provided by
the Asian Institute of Technology (AIT). The data, upon which the chapter is based, was
obtained from a variety of unpublished sources. The following organisations were most co-
operative: Bangkok Bank Limited; the Board of Trade of Thailand; the Department of
Industrial Promotion; the Department of Information; the Department of Technical and
Economic Co-operation; the Federation of Thai Industries; the Industrial Finance of Thailand;
Khon Kaen University; the Ministry of Commerce (including the Department of Business
Economics and the Department of Export Promotion); the National Economic and Social
Development Board; the Office of the Board of Investment; the Siam Commercial Bank; the
Thai Bankers Association, and the Thailand Development Research Institute.

163

Compared to their counterparts elsewhere, entrepreneurs in Thailand have been given greater leeway, and this has resulted in a vibrant entrepreneurial verve, reinforced by the Thai interpretation of Buddhist values. Thailand has long had a free-market culture, and entrepreneurs, along with their efficient work force, have contributed greatly to the Thai economy. Yet, while multinationals have been in the limelight, the potential of entrepreneurs has been underestimated.

Historical Overview

The original Thai kingdom came into existence in 1220, as a result of a Thai rebellion against the Khmers. King Ramkhamhaeng, who reigned from 1278 to 1318, adapted the Khmer alphabet to the Thai language. Monks from Ceylon were brought in to form a different form of Buddhism than that practised by the Khmers. The Thais subsequently adopted the Hinayana School of Orthodox Buddhism. When Ayutthaya was the national capital of the Thais (1358-1767), it was known as the Baghdad of the East – a thriving area for trade. Merchants reported that it was larger than was London at the time.

During the nineteenth century, the Thai kingdom – known as Siam, at the time – ceded some land to Britain (currently the north of peninsular Malaysia) and to France (currently part of Cambodia and Laos). Nevertheless, Siam succeeded in being the only country in the region to escape European colonial rule.

The country became a constitutional monarchy in 1932. In 1939, Siam changed its name to Thailand. During the next several decades, Thailand received considerable assistance from the United States. In 1991, Thailand embarked on a programme of economic deregulation and liberalisation.

The Influence of Buddhism in Thailand

Buddhism is more than a religion in the Western sense; it is also a philosophical system. With 94% of Thais being Buddhist, this way of life dominates culture and society in Thailand. Yet, since tolerance is central to Buddhist beliefs, Buddhism has never led to fanaticism or religious war.

© 1999 by Leo Paul Dana

Traditional Thai Dancers

Buddhism's tolerance has also allowed the survival of ancient Thai beliefs. Thus, Buddhism, as it is practised in Thailand, coexists with beliefs in omens. Stars and spirits are principal forces in daily life. Entrepreneurs consult astrologers – many of them self-employed Chinese – to determine the most auspicious time to expand their firms. Similar to the eye in Arab countries, or to garlic in Greece or Turkey, amulets are said to protect the Thais from misfortune.

Every factory, every store and every office in Thailand is expected to have a spirit house. This is an ornate, miniature temple, where spirits can be comfortable. This applies to all business enterprises – even brothels. In contrast to Christianity, which links sensual pleasure to sin, Buddhism involves a partnership of piety and pleasure. While good spirits do no harm, entrepreneurs often fear that bad spirits may hurt their business. To counter this, tattoos are used to keep away bad spirits.

The same philosophical system contributes greatly to entrepreneurship in Thailand, as it instils values that appear to encourage entrepreneurial spirit. The importance of tolerance extends beyond religion, to a respect for business competition.

Likewise, the prevalent philosophy in Thailand discourages abuse and envy. Buddhism in Thailand encourages: (i) asceticism; (ii) self-reliance; (iii) taking initiative; (iv) love of work; (v) diligence; (vi) patience; (vii) frugality; and (viii) efficiency. These qualities are very compatible with entrepreneurship:

(i) Since a young age, Thais are taught that Buddha left the comforts of his home to live a life of asceticism. The importance of asceticism is not unique to Buddhism. Weber (1904-5) linked entrepreneurship to asceticism.

(ii) Self-reliance is emphasised through Buddha's teaching, "Make of yourself a light. Rely upon yourself. Do not depend upon anyone else." Indeed, many Thais become self-employed, not to depend on others for employment. Bandura (1982) and Bandura and Adams (1977) reported a correlation between self-efficacy and subsequent task performance.

(iii) Buddha noted that people believing that everything happens by chance consequently lose hope and neglect to act wisely. Likewise, teachings discourage the belief in destiny, as the existence of destiny would imply that human plans and efforts for improvement and innovation would be in vain. Thais are taught not to rely on chance or fate. Instead, it is important to take initiative. There is an emphasis on an internal locus-of-control. Hull, Bosley and Udell (1980) found a correlation between an internal locus-of-control and entrepreneurial activity. Brockhaus (1982) and Begley and Boyd (1987) contended that entrepreneurs have a more internally oriented locus-of-control, than do non-entrepreneurs.

(iv) The teachings of Buddha specify that foolish people are avaricious for good results, but are too timid to go after them, and therefore fail. This is interpreted as emphasising the importance of a strong work ethic. Like asceticism, Weber (1904-5) linked work ethic to entrepreneurship.

(v) It is said that a man, who is satisfied with the progress he has made by little effort, relaxes his effort and becomes proud and conceited, falling into idleness and failure. This teaches people the importance of continuous efforts and determination. Hornaday (1982) noted that perseverance and determination are among the entrepreneurial characteristics most reported in academic surveys.

(vi) It is explained that a farmer cannot expect to see buds today, plants tomorrow and harvest the day after. The Thais learn that patience is a virtue.

(vii) King Udayana once asked Ananda what he was going to do with 500 garments he had just received. Ananda replied:

> I am going to distribute them among my brothers in rags.
> What will you do with the old garments?
> We will make bed covers out of them.
> What will you do with the old bed covers?
> We will make pillowcases.
> What will you do with the old pillowcases?
> We will make floor covers out of them.
> What will you do with the old floor covers?
> Use them for foot towels.
> And the old foot towels?
> Use them for floor mats.
> And the old ones?
> Tear them into pieces, and
> Mix them with mud and plaster the house-walls.

The moral of the parable is that frugality is desirable. Again, frugality is a quality that Weber (1904-5) linked to entrepreneurship.

(viii) Buddhism, as it is taught in Thailand, also teaches the importance of efficiency. A parable recounts the story of a traveller who came across an obstacle to his journey: a river. He therefore built a raft and safely crossed the river. Upon reaching the other bank, the man decided that despite its weight, he would keep the raft, "I will not abandon it to rot, but will carry it with me." Buddha explained that this was not efficient. Even a valuable asset should be discarded, when the cost of keeping it is greater than the benefit it provides.

© 1999 by Leo Paul Dana

Bangkok: A Venice of the East

Public Policy on Entrepreneurship in Thailand

The Royal Thai Government has long recognised the value of private investment in a free market economy with minimal government interference. Yet, support for entrepreneurs is a relatively recent phenomenon.

Early Economic Development Plans

The first National Economic Development Plan of Thailand (1961-1966) was greatly biased in favour of large enterprises. Its goal was to stimulate economic growth by providing large-scale investments via the Board of Investment and the Industrial Finance Corporation of Thailand.

Small-scale enterprises were given limited encouragement. The governor of Udorn helped small-scale farmers by introducing sorghum to them. While rice sold for 100 baht ($5 US at the time) per acre and required 210 days to mature, sorghum needed only 90 days to yield 200 baht per acre.

Eventually, policy-makers identified the need to upgrade existing small-scale enterprises, and in 1966, the Small Industry Service Institute was formed. Supported by the United Nations Development Programme (UNDP), its purpose was to provide technical assistance in order to modernise small-scale industries in Thailand.

Thailand's second economic development plan (1967-1971) largely replicated the first. Industrial estates were provided for small-scale industries, outside Bangkok. However, no assistance was provided to entrepreneurs.

The third economic development plan (1972-1976) perpetuated the concern with the importance of relocating industries outside the capital city. Incentives were promised. However, the oil crisis and the recession, which it caused, both contributed to delays.

The Board of Investment

The year 1977 witnessed the Investment Promotion Act, which developed the legal foundation for Thailand's Board of Investment. This government agency was empowered to grant preferential status to enterprises engaged in a variety of designated activities which were singled out including agriculture (see Exhibit 13.1); mining and related industries (see Exhibit 13.2); heavy industry (see Exhibit 13.3); manufacturing (see Exhibit 13.4); and services (see Exhibit 13.5).

• Animal feed	• Oil production from agricultural produce
• Animal products	
• Corn produce	• Processing of agricultural produce
• Cultivation of mulberry trees	• Processing or preservation of food
• Deep-sea and off-shore fishing	• Production of milk powder
• Large-scale cultivation	• Production of soybeans and complete refinement of oil
• Livestock raising	
• Manufacture of products made from bamboo, for export	• Products from stick lac
	• Rabbit raising and processing, for export
• Manufacture of products made from rattan, for export	• Rubber products
• Manufacture of products made from palm leaf, for export	• Silk reeling and/or spinning
	• Silk worm farming
• Multiplication of vegetable seeds	• Slaughter of cattle

Exhibit 13.1: Agricultural Products and Commodities Eligible
for Special Status in Thailand[17]

---

[17] Source: Board of Investment, Bangkok, Thailand.

170 *Entrepreneurship in Pacific Asia: Past, Present & Future*

• Acetylene black products	• Paints
• Carbon black	• Petrochemicals
• Carbon paste products	• Petroleum products
• Ceramic products	• Pharmaceuticals
• Chemical products	• Pulp and paper products
• Fertilisers	• Rayon grade pulp
• Metal products	• Salt products
• Mineral ore prospecting	• Smelting
• Mining	• Soda ash

Exhibit 13.2: Minerals, Metals, Chemical Products and Ceramics Eligible for Special Status in Thailand[18]

• Assembly of electronic goods
• Assembly of engines or other mechanical or electrical equipment
• Production of components of machinery or electrical equipment
• Production of electronic goods
• Production of engines or other mechanical or electrical equipment
• Production of oil drilling platforms
• Production of vehicle parts

Exhibit 13.3: Mechanical and Electrical Equipment Eligible for Special Status in Thailand[19]

---

[18] Source: Board of Investment, Bangkok, Thailand.
[19] Source: Board of Investment, Bangkok, Thailand.

• Abrasive sheets	• Medical or scientific equipment
• Adhesive tape products	• Natural fibre products
• Aqueous electrolytic cell cases and parts, for export	• Non-dairy creamer products
• Arms and ammunitions	• Ornaments for wear
• Artificial flowers and trees, for export	• Packaging products
• Boats and ships	• Plastic or plastic-coated products
• Cameras	• Prefabricated housing components
• Carpets	• Printed textiles
• Caskets	• Products for export
• Cellophane	• Rubber soles
• Clocks or watches or components thereof	• Medical supplies
• Coated aluminium sheets for printing	• Musical instruments
• Cutting and polishing of gem stones	• Rubber tree products
• Fire hydrants or components thereof	• Scale ice
• Flat glass products for use in construction	• Shaving equipment
• Foamed glass or products thereof	• Shipyards
• Glass fibre or products thereof	• Showcases
• Gloves	• Socks
• Grinding wheels	• Soft gelatine capsule products
• Hand tools	• Sporting equipment
• Knitted products	• Stationery, educational equipment or parts thereof
• Lenses, spectacles and parts thereof	• Synthetic fibre products
• Matches for export	• Toys
• Measuring and testing equipment	• Tyre cords
	• Umbrellas
	• Wall cloth covering products
	• Woven products
	• Yarns
	• Zips

Note: Products not listed may be eligible if considered to be of "great benefit" to the national economy and in accordance with national development objectives.

Exhibit 13.4: Other Products Eligible for Special Status in Thailand[20]

---

[20] Source: Board of Investment, Bangkok, Thailand.

- Agricultural export centres
- Air transportation
- Car parking
- Cold storage
- Commercial airports
- Concession expressways
- Container repair, maintenance and refurbishment
- Container yards
- Convention halls
- Crop drying
- Disinfecting services for exports
- Ferryboat service
- Grading facilities for agricultural produce
- Hospitals
- Hotels
- Industrial estates
- International trade show centres
- International trading
- Loading and unloading facilities for sea transport
- Mass transit systems
- Modern packaging of produce for export
- Modern rice processing
- Motion picture film processing
- Production or sale of water for industrial use
- Repair services for vehicles, machinery or engines
- Research and development
- Selected ship services
- Service centres for the petrochemical industry
- Silo facilities
- Tourism promotion
- Transport of natural gas
- Transport of water
- Warehousing
- X-ray computer services

Exhibit 13.5: Services Eligible for Special Status in Thailand[21]

---

[21] Source: Board of Investment, Bangkok, Thailand.

Projects attracting the most generous incentive packages include:

- those expected to generate substantial employment;
- those located outside Bangkok;
- those which conserved energy;
- those which involved substitutes for imported fuel;
- those with the potential for foreign exchange earnings; and
- those deemed complementary to the development of basic industries.

Qualifying entrepreneurs may be granted exemptions from import duties, from withholding taxes and from income tax. In addition, the Investment Promotion Act empowered the Board of Investment to provide guarantees against competition from new state enterprises. Finally, tariff protection may be introduced, and in some cases, the products of foreign competitors may be banned.

The Board of Investment evolved over time. In its early years, it served as an incentive-granting agency, dedicating much of its resources to monitoring the tax incentives granted to enterprises. Eventually, it established a "One Stop Centre" and took on the role of business advisor, providing technical expertise to entrepreneurs.

Changing Priorities

Like its predecessor, Thailand's fourth economic development plan (1977-1981) was also concerned with the importance of relocating industries outside Bangkok. However, the facilities in the estates continued to be minimal, and operating costs were high. This situation prompted a shift in priorities.

The fifth economic development plan (1982-1986) ushered in a new era for Thailand, marking a shift in policy direction. This time, the government emphasised the need to promote small-scale industry as the pillar of industrial development in Thailand. Policy-makers expected that providing specific incentives to small-scale enterprises would result in these firms growing faster than the rate of growth among large corporations. Also, if small firms were concentrated outside the nation's capital, then growth would be decentralised outside Bangkok. This new approach was consistent with the state's long-term objective of narrowing the gap between Bangkok and the less developed regions of the country.

The state-owned Transport Company, Ltd. controlled 10% of the total traffic on buses linking Bangkok and the provinces. In a bold move, this company gave franchises to local entrepreneurs. This turned out to be highly profitable for the franchiser, as well as the franchisees.

During the mid-1980s, large enterprises achieved unexpected success in expanding their export performance. This prompted policy-makers to change their strategy again. Rather than providing policies to promote small industries, it was decided to focus on promoting exports. Consequently, Thailand's sixth economic development plan (1987-1991) was not concerned with small firms.

Major Reform

In September 1990, the Royal Thai Government reduced tariffs on machinery, from 20% to 5%. This stimulated latent demand among price-elastic entrepreneurs, thereby facilitating the transfer of technology.

In January 1991, the Royal Thai Government agreed to create a free trade area and to reduce tariffs among the members of the Association of South East Asian Nations (ASEAN), at the time consisting of Brunei, Indonesia, Malaysia, the Philippines, Singapore and Thailand. Later that year, Prime Minister Anand Panyarachun introduced economic reforms, and streamlined several government bureaus, in order to open Thailand to competition.

Of particular concern to entrepreneurs was the structure of the tax system at the time. Personal income tax rates were very high, especially compared to those in neighbouring Malaysia. Furthermore, the cascading nature of the business tax discouraged backward linkages. Consequently, a Value Added Tax (VAT) was introduced in January 1992, replacing the old system of business taxes. In April 1992, Thailand announced that it wanted to slow down tariff cuts to which it had agreed the previous year.

Making Entrepreneurship Central to Industry

Propelled by manufactured exports, Thailand became the world's fastest growing economy. A problem, however, was that the manufacturing sector became top heavy, *i.e.* strong in final assembly but less so in supply industries. This led to a bottleneck, as firms developed a dependence on imported raw materials and machinery. Supply and support industries have a major impact on a nation's industrial sector, because their role is to feed manufacturing operations.

Thailand's seventh economic development plan (1992-1996) explicitly emphasised a commitment to the rapid development of key support industries, and this was of special interest to entrepreneurs. Countless small firms are the core of the domestic support industries in Thailand. Yet, they often suffered from a lack of economy of scale or the lack of technology to be globally competitive. Although components could be produced in Thailand, local firms lacked the resources to produce the quantities for which demand existed. Therefore, the Board of Investment implemented a special programme to promote the growth of small and medium scale Thai companies in the area of support industries. The Board of Investment Unit for Industrial Linkage Development (BUILD) devised a scheme to market the concept of backward linkages to smaller firms, whereby small firms acquire technology from multinationals, in order to supply them with components.

In recent years, the Bank of Thailand and also the Industrial Finance Corporation of Thailand have given preferential financial assistance to entrepreneurs. Priority has been focused on rural entrepreneurs using local raw materials to produce exports.

The Financial Crisis in Thailand

In early 1996, the baht was showing signs of weakness. In July 1997, the Thai baht collapsed, prompting a domino effect across the Far East. Almost 2 million people lost their jobs and unemployment surged from almost nil, to 6%.

In November 1997, a new coalition government was elected, headed by Prime Minister Chuan Leekpai. He proved himself an honest man, eager to implement economic reforms proposed by the International Monetary Fund, along with a $17.2 billion US package.

Within a few months, the Royal Thai Government closed over 50 finance companies, nationalised four failing banks, and opened the financial industry to foreigners. These government actions were followed by an announcement that Bangchak Petroleum, Thai Airways International and the Electricity Generating Authority of Thailand were scheduled to be at least partially privatised. Not surprisingly, this led to opposition from labour. Meanwhile, the Asian Development Bank led a consortium of banks which lent $1 billion US to Thai exporters.

In 1998, the Royal Thai Cabinet approved the Industrial Restructuring Master Plan, prepared by the Ministry of Industry. This involved strategies to do the following:

- move towards production of higher value-added products for middle-to-higher markets with higher quality standards by upgrading technology and quality management and developing product designs in line with market preferences.
- improve efficiency in terms of production costs, streamline production processes and improve delivery and quick response.
- create production and trading alliances to enhance technology transfer and expand marketing channels.
- reduce industrial pollution.
- disperse industrial employment to regional and rural areas.
- upgrade the knowledge and skills of the industrial workforce.[22]

The National Economic and Social Development Bureau, which is the economic planning body of Thailand, prepared a privatisation plan, to shift economic functions from the state to private enterprises. The Council of Economic Ministers of the Royal Thai Government endorsed this plan, promising a bright future for entrepreneurs in Thailand.

---

[22] Source: Mr. Manu Leopairote, Director-General, Department of Industrial Promotion, Ministry of Industry, Royal Thai Government.

Foreign Assistance for Entrepreneurs

In addition to enjoying an enterprise-friendly public policy, which has been supportive of entrepreneurship, Thai entrepreneurs have long benefited from a variety of foreign aid programmes. It was mentioned earlier that the Small Industry Service Institute was founded in 1966.

With financial assistance from the International Labour Organisation and from the United Nations Special Fund, the Small Industries Service Institute evolved into the Industrial Services Division of the Ministry of Industry's Department of Industrial Promotion. Initially, its scope was to modernise small-scale industries across the board; by the 1990s its mandate was to focus on enterprises in specific sectors, regardless of firm size.

The Industrial Services Division was organised into three sub-divisions, namely (i) the Furniture Industry Sub-Division; (ii) the Miscellaneous Industries Sub-Division; and (iii) the Design Promotion Sub-Division. This allowed the Division to allocate its resources across six industrial sectors: (i) furniture; (ii) agro-industry; (iii) jewellery; (iv) packaging; (v) toys; and (vi) industrial design. These sectors were selected because they were "particularly beneficial" to the industrial and economic development of the nation.

Entrepreneurs and potential entrepreneurs interested in the above sectors are entitled to a wide range of services from the Industrial Services Division. These include training courses, seminars, exhibitions, technology, acquisition, product testing, analysis, design promotion, consultancy and industrial studies.

Another important contributor has been the International Fund for Agricultural Development, which began making loans and giving grants to self-employed small-scale farmers in Thailand, in 1978. Earning its reputation as the "rice bowl" of Asia, Thailand has become an important exporter of food. Principal crops include cassava, kenaf, maize, rice and rubber.

Individual nations have also made contributions. The Canadian International Development Assistance (CIDA) programme, for example, established the Small and Medium Enterprise (SME) Project to support the growth of SMEs in north-eastern Thailand. This programme has included the provision of credit as well as advisory services. The SME Project has been administered through the Royal Thai Department of Industrial Promotion.

CIDA also designed the Northeast Fisheries Project, to assist small-scale fishing operations.   Additionally, CIDA has funded a community-based Integrated Rural Development project, helping small-scale farmers and cottage industries.   Finally, CIDA launched the Enterprise Collaboration Project, aimed to support joint ventures between Canadian and Thai entrepreneurs.

© 1999 by Leo Paul Dana

A Cottage Industry: Elephant Carving

Ethnic-Chinese Entrepreneurs in Thailand

Chinese traders have long been active in Thailand. This is especially so in Bangkok, the nation's main port. Two groups of ethnic-Chinese became prominent – the Hokkiens and the Teochews. The former spoke Minnanhua – a dialect from Fujian province – while the latter spoke Chaozhouhua – a dialect from Guang Dong province. Hokkiens found employment as tax collectors for the royal family, during the eighteenth century. Teochews became entrepreneurs.

Throughout the twentieth century, more ethnic-Chinese entrepreneurs migrated to Thailand, and became prominent in business. Whereas religious and cultural differences prevented the Chinese from assimilating smoothly into Muslim countries, this was not the case in Thailand. A common religion (Buddhism) and the lack of discrimination helped them blend into Thai society. Unlike Burma, Indonesia, Malaysia and Vietnam, Thailand never favoured its indigenous people at the expense of the ethnic-Chinese community. As explained by respondents interviewed by the author, "We don't feel any different whether they are Thai or Chinese." Thailand's tolerance of entrepreneurship, in its Chinese community, contributed to a healthy national economy. In 1999, 14% of Thailand's population was Chinese, and ethnic-Chinese entrepreneurs controlled 90% of manufacturing in Thailand (Yeung, 1999).

Through marriage to Thai women, Chinese men integrated well into their host society, and it became fashionable to adopt Thai names. Barth (1981) argued that when two groups interact, they begin sharing values. In the case of Thailand, although the government limited the number of Chinese schools, the community preserved its cultural values, a desire for education and its diligent work ethic. Silcock (1967) described the Chinese of Thailand as the "Jews of the East."

The most powerful Chinese family used to be the Tejapaibul family, with their banking, distilling and real estate empire. Chin Sophonpanich, owner of hospitals and plantations and father of the Bangkok Bank, was a prominent leader of the Chinese community in Bangkok, until his death in 1988. Also among the prominent ethnic Chinese entrepreneurs, in Thailand, is Chan Ratanarak.

Chan Ratanarak was born in China in 1920, and was brought to Thailand by his parents, in 1926. In 1945, he was still a wage-worker at the port of Bangkok. He then established his own firm, loading sea vessels. In time, he progressed to banking and manufacturing, as did numerous ethnic-Chinese entrepreneurs in Thailand. By the 1990s, he controlled the Bank of Ayudhya and Siam City Cement.

Other important families of Chinese entrepreneurs in Thailand include the Chearavanonts, the Chokwatanas and the Shinawatras. The Chearavanonts established the Charoen Pokphand (CP) group. This involved animal feed, petrochemicals and a joint venture with British Telecom. Thiam Chokwatana started out with one shop in 1942. This evolved into the Saha Pathana group, including 60 companies producing a variety of goods from clothing to detergents. Although a third of these came to be listed on the stockmarket, each of Chokwatana's sons has kept control of at least one listed corporation. The family business proved to be very successful, despite competition from Colgate, Procter & Gamble and Unilever. Thaksin Shinawatra, an ethnic-Chinese from Chiang Mai, started out as a distributor of IBM computers. He later set up a cable-television network and then decided to establish his own cellular telephone operation.

More than half of Bangkok's seven million people are of Chinese ancestry. They tend to be very active in entrepreneurship. They are involved in a wide range of activities, from manufacturing to retailing. Some are bakers. Others are self-employed astrologists and palmists, respected occupations in this superstitious society. Entrepreneurs in Bangkok's Chinatown tend to sell cloth, gold and noodles.

© 1999 by Leo Paul Dana

In addition, hundreds of entrepreneurs from Taiwan have been contributing to foreign direct investment across Thailand. There are about 8 million ethnic-Chinese in Thailand. Although they comprise only 14% of Thailand's population, they control four fifths of the market capital in Thailand. Fifty-six percent of them are Teochew.

© 1999 by Leo Paul Dana
Selling Bananas at a Floating Market

Women Entrepreneurs in Thailand

Although Thai women are often portrayed as being subservient to men, Thai culture fosters a relatively egalitarian status for men and women. According to the culture, both genders are equally important.

Traditionally, Thai women have had leadership roles in community health, education and earning family income. More recently, women have become very visible in Thailand's entrepreneurship sector. Many are owner-managers of small firms. Others own enterprises which have grown into larger-scale businesses.

One woman entrepreneur owns a golf course. Another – this one from Chiang Mai – operates a large antique business. Women operate a bus company in Bangkok, along with a fleet of ferryboats.

Toward the Future

Several development plans have recognised the potential of entrepreneurs; yet, programmes to foster entrepreneurship have been over-shadowed by politics encouraging multinationals. In some cases, this has been at the expense of local entrepreneurship.

During the latter decades of the twentieth century, Thailand became an export base for multinationals, which enjoyed low labour costs in an open economy. However, little was done to supply these corporations from within Thailand. Therefore, much production activity was little more than assembly work.

In the twenty-first century, the use of local suppliers will increase cost-effectiveness for multinationals, while allowing local entrepreneurship to play an increasingly vital role in the Thai economy. The regional economy will also contribute to entrepreneurship in Thailand. Already, Thai entrepreneurs have been engaging in business with Laos and Myanmar.

© 1999 by Leo Paul Dana

Protecting the Monarchy

© 1999 by Leo Paul Dana

Convenient Urban Transportation: A Tuk-Tuk

Chapter 14

The "Market Socialist Economy" of Vietnam[23]

Introduction

The Socialist Republic of Vietnam covers 331,668 square kilometres, is bordered by Cambodia, Laos and China. Until the 1980s, Vietnam had an economic policy in line with the market substitution model – a dominant strategy in much of the Third World up to the late 1960s. According to this model, the means to national economic development was to manufacture consumer goods locally, thereby replacing imports. This approach necessitated the existence of high tariffs, quotas or other regulatory mechanisms to discourage importation of goods. These policies, in turn, often encouraged industrialisation, but resulted in over-diversified manufacturing rather than specialisation along the lines of competitive advantage. A frequent problem with this model is the creation of a highly protected, high cost, but low quality and inefficient industrial sector. Furthermore, exports were usually biased against, due to a typically overvalued official currency exchange rate.

---

[23] The author researched this chapter in Vietnam. Transportation to Vietnam was provided by McGill University. The contents are based on unpublished documents and in-depth interviews conducted at a variety of bureaus, including the Central Bureau of Statistics, the Committee of Foreign Economic Affairs, the Export Development Trading Corporation, the Foreign Trade Development Centre, and the Planning and Trading Department of Artex-Saigon. In addition, National Congress documents were consulted. Some of the subject matter has appeared in earlier publications by the author.

In response to the situation existing at the time, Vietnam moved away from import substitution and experimented with its own model of reform – *Doi-Moi.*

Economic policy in Vietnam aimed to create that which the state referred to as "a market socialist economy." In the attempt to ensure domestic growth, the Socialist Republic of Vietnam implemented a drastic programme of economic reform. Those regulations, which formerly limited the private sector, were substantially reduced, and Vietnam moved away from being a very highly centralised command economy. On July 29, 1995, Vietnam became a member of ASEAN. However, the government *never* rejected socialist ideology. Rather than rushing to privatise state firms, the government concentrated its efforts on agricultural development, the rural economy and the domestic market. What still concerns Taiwanese entrepreneurs, who invested in Vietnam, is the direction of government policy. Specifically, these individuals expressed concern about the recent introduction of exchange controls. Vietnam should take these concerns seriously, as the Taiwanese form the largest group of investors in Vietnam.

Historical Overview

Tonkin, the northern part of Vietnam, was originally inhabited by Indonesian peoples. As a result of Chinese invasion, it became a province of the Chinese Empire, from the year 42 AD until the fall of the T'ang dynasty. This land subsequently became independent in 938, but reverted to Chinese rule from 1407 until 1427.

Further south was the Kingdom of Champa (central Vietnam), founded in the third century. It eventually fell under the control of Vietnam, which was expanding from the north. After a lengthy civil war, the Vietnamese kingdom was split into two in 1660, when the Nguyen family established their own separate kingdom.

The extreme south of Vietnam, known as Cochin-China, remained under Cambodian rule until a century later. Finally, the whole of Vietnam was unified in 1802, by the Nguyen dynasty. Its capital was Hué, situated in the northern part of the area later to become known as South Vietnam.

The North Vietnamese are of a Sino-Tibetan race with Han culture; the people of the south have a history of mixing with Polynesian races who tend to have been exposed to slightly more Dionysian and fewer Promethian values. While the people of the north adopted a northern sect of Buddhism, those of Cochin-China included followers of a southern sect of Buddhism with some Hindu influence.

In order to protect persecuted Catholic missionaries in Vietnam, France invaded the south in 1859, changing the status of the latter in 1867, to the colony of French Cochin-China. In 1885, France established a protectorate over Tonkin and the middle of Vietnam. All of Vietnam thus became part of *Indochine française* (French Indo-China).

The Hoa – a significant ethnic-Chinese minority – were very active in the small business sector; the French, not wanting to deal directly with the Vietnamese, encouraged the Hoa to serve as "middleman" entrepreneurs, and these continued to dominate sectors of the economy. (Auster and Aldrich (1984), Bonacich (1973), Cherry (1990), and Dana (1997d) discuss middleman entrepreneurship in detail.)

From 1941 to 1945, Japan occupied Vietnam. Then, Nguyen That Thanh, calling himself Ho Chi Minh (literally meaning "the brilliant one"), declared himself president of newly independent Vietnam. France sent its forces to re-assert French rule, and by 1946 France had regained control of its former colony of Cochin-China, but not of its former protectorate to the north.

© 1999 by Leo Paul Dana

The French Introduced the *Baguette* to Saigon

© 1999 by Leo Paul Dana

The French Brought European Cars with Them

In 1954, an armistice agreement, in Geneva, created the Democratic Republic of Vietnam (North Vietnam) north of the 17th parallel, and the Republic of Vietnam (South Vietnam) to its south. Hanoi, formerly the administrative capital of Indo-China, became the capital of North Vietnam. Saigon became the capital of South Vietnam.

The communist Viet Minh took control of North Vietnam, under the leadership of Ho Chi Minh. His government instituted a programme of land reform. Consequently, several hundred thousand small-scale land-owners fled from the north to the south. Only in South Vietnam could the spirit of entrepreneurship survive. In North Vietnam, the First Five-Year Plan, 1961-1965, put emphasis on basic heavy industries and continued to influence industrial policy until the 1980s. (The second plan would not be drawn up until 1976.)

Despite American efforts to assure the independence of South Vietnam, the communists overran the country in 1975. The following year saw the creation of the Socialist Republic of Vietnam, consisting of a politically united country, with Hanoi as its capital. Despite political unification, regional differences remained strong.

The introduction of centralised planning from North Vietnam, into the market economy of South Vietnam, resulted in a drop in rice and livestock production. With the new regime came a drop of foreign exchange, resulting in a shortage of imported inputs, new materials and spare parts. This, in turn, was the cause of an under-utilisation of capacity, as domestic supply could not satisfy consumer demand. Further constraints in capacity utilisation were brought about by shortages in energy production and a weak transportation network, which received minimal maintenance and had seen virtually no improvements since the departure of the French in 1954.

Furthermore, state firms in the Socialist Republic of Vietnam lacked access to modern technology. Their costs of production were high, relative to the quality of their products, which were considered to be low by international standards.

All firms in the south were nationalised, even the smallest businesses. Every bookstore in the country was shut down and inventories were confiscated. Government newspapers replaced the existing dailies. Private homes were raided and "decadent" literature was burned. As the Hanoi government tried to spread Marxist ideology, schools of bourgeois learning were closed.

With reunification, all bank accounts in former South Vietnam were frozen, and the South Vietnamese were told they had twelve hours to take their cash to the banks as such currency would become valueless. Henceforth, all of Vietnam would have one currency, but each family was limited to a maximum saving, the equivalent of approximately $200 US at the time.

At the fourth national congress of the communist party of Vietnam, it was declared that:

> The State of the Socialist Republic of Vietnam is a proletarian dictatorship state. On the one hand, it represses counter-revolutionaries, eliminates the comprador capitalist class and the remnants of the feudal landlord class, carries out socialist transformation of the... private capitalist economic element; at the same time it effects the socialist transformation of the private economic section (Chinh, 1977, p. 1).

On the Train Across Vietnam

Billboards Try to Promote Socialism

Government Policy in Vietnam

The Second Five-Year Plan (1976-1980) set a 16-18% targeted annual growth rate for industrial production; actual outcome was 0.6%. In 1978, the Sino-Vietnamese War prompted an exodus of ethnic-Chinese from Vietnam. In 1979 and 1980 there were shortages of basic consumer goods including food, as well as shortages of inputs to the industrial sector.

It was liberalisation, in 1981, which helped industrial output to grow an average of over 9% during the period of the Third Five-Year Plan (1981-1985). Growth was primarily generated by small and medium-sized enterprises, some in the private sector. This was made possible by the Three-Plan System introduced in 1981:

1. Plan A: Enterprises operating under this scheme were required to produce using state-supplied inputs and to sell their outputs to the state at low command prices.

2. Plan B: This scheme permitted firms to acquire inputs on their own, and to sell their outputs independently, provided that the profits were used to purchase additional inputs.

3. Plan C: This scheme permitted entrepreneurs to diversify and to sell "minor" products with no centrally planned external control.

In 1982, the Fifth Party Congress officially adopted its new economic orientation, recognising the need to:

(i)   shift emphasis from heavy to light industry;
(ii)   transfer resources to the agricultural sector; and
(iii)   promote exports.

As production activities were partially deregulated, individual enterprises were granted some autonomy. In 1984, the government further relaxed restrictions.

When a new currency was introduced, in 1985, old dong were exchanged at a rate of 10:1, but only up to a set quantity. Also in 1985, consumer price subsidies were replaced by wage adjustments. Most prices remained under central control, determined by an average cost-plus formula; however, some costs were not accurately assessed.

The nation's economic development followed an import substitution model. Industrial policy in Vietnam was influenced by that of the former Soviet Union. Centrally planned industrialisation was aimed at the domestic production of heavy industry such as capital goods. The state supplied the input and capital requirements of enterprises and set quantitative output targets. Policy typically leaned towards achieving self-sufficiency, but neglected opportunities for trade.

Several problems with this model led to the realisation that changes would be necessary. The attempt to be self-sufficient had led to insufficient specialisation. Investment had been scattered over too many projects, without priority or complementarity. Despite substantial vertical integration, there was a lack of horizontal integration. Entrepreneurship was restricted by regulation coupled with excessive bureaucratic centralisation. Innovation and creativity were stifled. Research, science and technology for industry were weak. Energy supplies were lacking. Export-oriented activities were not being given enough attention and there were insufficient links between foreign markets and Vietnamese producers; the latter lacked awareness about international quality, prices and demands. There was more incentive for a farmer to chop down a tree and use it for firewood than to harvest the fruit. Aggravating the situation for producers in Vietnam, were the constant limitations on capital resources and raw material supplies, especially those that were imported. Construction periods were typically overrun and numerous projects remained unfinished. Reform, or more specifically "renovation" became a necessity.

Major change was introduced towards the end of December 1986, when the Sixth Congress of the National Representatives of the Communist Party approved economic reforms that eliminated much of the basic apparatus of control. This programme was called *Doi-Moi*, literally, "Renovation." Individual entrepreneurs obtained the right to get involved in light industry. Profits were defined as the difference between the value of sales and *allowable* costs; enterprises remained liable for taxes on profits. Restrictions on wages were abolished and enterprises were given the right to recruit according to their needs.

In contrast to the experiences in Eastern Europe and in the former Soviet Union (where a market economy was decreed to have replaced communism without a long transition period), *Doi-Moi* was poised to evolve slowly, thereby ushering in entrepreneurship as a *complement* to state enterprise, rather than as a *replacement*.

In July 1988, The Resolution of New Regulation for the Non-State Economic Sector (Resolution No. 16) called for tapping the potential of entrepreneurs and turning them into important components of the national economy. Specifically, the resolution states that entrepreneurs:

- shall be permitted to operate independently of the central planning process of the state;
- shall have the option of procuring machinery and other equipment from state units, on an equal footing as state producers;
- shall have the option of purchasing technical training service and technology from state institutions;
- shall not be discriminated against by monopoly state organisations that supply inputs (*e.g.*, raw materials, spare parts, technology, etc.);
- shall have the right to obtain inputs independently from monopoly state organisations, dealing directly with other independent entrepreneurs;
- who wish to export may elect to choose their own independent sales outlets;
- who export may negotiate their own foreign sales contracts;
- who export successfully may use their foreign exchange to import capital goods such as machinery and other equipment from abroad; and
- shall be entitled to patent and copyright protection.

Government policy on forestry was also reformed, adjusting the respective roles of the Ministry of Forestry and the private sector. New legislation was introduced to:

- allow entrepreneurs to use assigned areas of forest for one to three rotations of a tree crop;
- develop forestry regulations and enforcement such as to prevent abusive exploitation;
- assist in developing forest product markets;
- evolve from the state forestry companies to a contract system; and
- tax marketed output.

On September 5, 1988, the Council of Ministries adopted Decree 139 Regulating in Detail the Implementation of the Law on Foreign Investment in Vietnam. This set forth detailed procedures and requirements relating to foreign investment and the corresponding tax structure.

In the case of a joint venture, the foreign party usually contributes hard currency and technology, while the Vietnamese party may participate with non-convertible currency and/or land. Vietnamese law also permits the Vietnamese partner to contribute water and sea surface rights.

A further breakthrough in the reintroduction of market-oriented policies followed in 1989, when the predominantly rural population was granted the right of access to land and the right to sell output at market prices. Furthermore, the right for the access to land could be inherited. Whereas Vietnam had been near starvation prior to this reform, the nation soon became the world's third largest rice exporter (1.4 metric tonnes in 1992). Without abandoning Marxist ideals, young intellectuals came to the conclusion that a market economy with entrepreneurship and a private small business sector is the quickest means to attain the benefits sought out by socialism. The result has been a unique blend of socialist and free enterprise policies whereby the entrepreneur is the agent for social change as described by Barth (1963; 1967), but in a socialist state, *i.e.*, the government affirmed its commitment to free enterprise within the context of socialism. New billboards began to promote *Doi-Moi*, while others continued urging workers to follow socialism.

Most prices in Vietnam were released from centralised control, in 1989. Exceptions were electricity, petrol and transportation. This policy enabled entrepreneurs and the small business sector to begin setting prices as a function of market forces, while keeping energy and transportation costs artificially low, thus indirectly subsidising entrepreneurship. That same year, the State Committee for Co-operation and Investment was established, as the body responsible for foreign direct investment and for providing guidance to foreign entrepreneurs. Taiwanese entrepreneurs were among the first to arrive in Vietnam *en masse*.

© 1999 by Leo Paul Dana
Vietnam Became a Leading Rice Exporter

In 1990, the Ministry for External Economic Relations was absorbed into the Ministry of Commerce. The former had already issued about 100 permits to provincial and local enterprises (and a similar amount to central government firms) permitting them to export directly and allowing them to keep a substantial proportion of the foreign exchange earned. Also in 1990, the Council of Non-State Enterprises was established, specifically to promote the interests of entrepreneurs and the private small business sector, including the principles established by Resolution 16, two years earlier. Entrepreneurship and the small business sector in Vietnam began to flourish, with foreign as well as local entrepreneurs active in private business.

Very significant was Decree 28, adopted by the National Assembly on June 30, 1990, replacing former Decree 139. The new legislation was named the "Law on Amendments and Additions to a Number of Articles of the Law on Foreign Investment in Vietnam."

Relaxation of regulations made it possible for foreign entrepreneurs to hold 100% of the equity of a business in Vietnam. Furthermore, the Law of Foreign Investment protects capital property and other assets of foreign entrepreneurship from nationalisation. Foreign direct investment (FDI) cannot be expropriated or requisitioned by administrative procedure. Legislation also made new FDI ventures income tax exempt for the first four years of operations.

As well, foreign entrepreneurs operating in Vietnam were given the right to remit profits abroad as well as to remit payments abroad for the provision of technology, services and loans. In contrast to China, where only foreign exchange profits could be remitted abroad, Vietnam had no foreign exchange restrictions at the time. Therefore, according to Article 86 of the Foreign Investment Law, profits earned in Vietnam could be converted into hard currency at the Bank of Foreign Trade. These funds could then be repatriated, according to Article 87.

With Decision 25-CP, on January 21, 1991, Vietnam established that all enterprises belonging to the socialist state would develop plans directed by the market. A few months later, the Seventh Party Congress was held in Hanoi, June 24-27, 1991. On the agenda were concerns such as:

> serious inflation; unstable production; increasing unemployment; wages and salaries below subsistence level... widespread corruption and other evils... an erosion of cultural, spiritual and moral values; and declining confidence in the Party and the State (Communist Party of Vietnam, 1991, p. 150).

Confirming the leading role of the Communist Party, and its adherence to Marxist-Leninism, the Seventh National Party Congress renewed the strategy of *Doi-Moi*:

> The overall objectives of this strategy up to the year 2000 are to emerge from crisis, stabilise the socio-economic situation, strive to overcome the condition of poverty and underemployment, improve living conditions for the country to develop more rapidly in the early 21st century. Gross domestic product by the year 2000 will be double of that of 1990 (Communist Party of Vietnam, 1991, p. 157).

In June 1991, the Seventh Congress of the National Representatives of the Communist Party reaffirmed their commitment to *Doi-Moi*. In 1991, the Viet Kieu community (overseas Vietnamese), numbering 700,000 in the United States alone, contributed approximately half a billion US dollars to the Vietnamese economy.

© 1997 by Leo Paul Dana

Light Industry Under *Doi-Moi*

In 1992, the Labour Ministry announced a new reform aimed at encouraging foreign entrepreneurs to create jobs. The minimum wage for employees of foreign entrepreneurs was *reduced* to $30 US monthly. Also in 1992, the government began the process of privatising state enterprises. The first state enterprise to be offered for sale to the private sector was the Legamex garment factory, run by Ms. Nguyen Thi Son in Ho Chi Minh City. In 1992, Legamex exported 1,700,000 jackets to Germany.

According to government statistics, in 1992 some 700 major state enterprises, under the control of the central government, were mostly involved in heavy industry. Another 2,300 locally-controlled state firms were concentrated primarily in light industry.

Heavy industries, including cement, chemicals, engines, fertiliser, iron and steel, are concentrated in the north; lighter industries are concentrated in the south where individual entrepreneurs are also directly involved.

A tight economic policy succeeded in reducing inflation from over 700% in 1986, to 70% in 1990, 68% in 1991, 18% in 1992 and to about 10% in 1993. Per capita GDP in 1992 was $125 US. After the United States dropped its trade embargo, per capita income jumped from $190 in 1994, to $275 the following year.

In July 1995, Vietnam became the seventh member of ASEAN. Also in 1995, the National Assembly adopted a new Civil Code, which laid the foundation for a market economy. That same year, import duties of 60% were reduced.

The Eighth Congress of the Representatives of the Communist Party took place in June 1996. The 1996-2000 plan called for $21 billion US, in foreign investment, to complement $21 billion in local investments.

In 1997, Vietnam's exports grew by 24%, while inflation was 4%. Although the Vietnamese dong depreciated by about 20% compared to the dollar, exports grew by only 3.5% between January and October 1998. Inflation approached 10%. The Asian Crisis had hit Vietnam, and this was of concern to the state's Central Committee, which convened in October 1998, to outline an economic strategy for 1999.

In contrast to government policy that had, in recent years, designated entrepreneurs as economic engines of growth, the Central Committee decided that state-owned enterprises would lead the Vietnamese economy, giving priority to the local market. The state was not in a rush to privatise state firms, nor to reform the almost obsolete banking sector. Instead, the government decided to focus its efforts, in 1999, on agricultural development, the rural economy and the domestic market.

Building a Financial Infrastructure

Under communist rule, individuals in Vietnam were traditionally unable to have bank accounts. Although the *Doi-Moi* model allowed the development of entrepreneurship in Vietnam, entrepreneurial activity was constrained by a tight money supply and by the absence of a modern financial infrastructure. The state-owned banks favoured state-owned firms.

Up to 1988, Vietnam's monolithic banking structure was a tripod, with the State Bank of Vietnam directly controlling the Bank for Foreign Trade and the Construction and Investment Bank. While the Construction and Investment Bank handled domestic financial matters, the Bank for Foreign Trade handled credit transactions involving foreign exchange. Eventually, these various financial institutions became autonomous.

A commercial banking decree, "Decree on Banks, Credit Co-operative and Financial Companies," was promulgated by the Council of Ministers in May 1990. This edict set forth conditions and procedures for establishing commercial banking in Vietnam.

Simultaneously, the "Decree on the State Bank of Vietnam" appointed the State Bank of Vietnam as the central monetary authority of the nation. This empowered the State Bank to issue currency, set exchange rates, and supervise banking transactions of the autonomous commercial banks.

In July 1992, *Banque Indosuez* of France and Bangkok Bank of Thailand became the first two foreign banks to open branches in Ho Chi Minh City (formerly Saigon). By 1993, ANZ had a branch in Hanoi as well as a representative office in Ho Chi Minh City. Other banks, which were quick to enter Vietnam, included Banque Nationale de Paris, Credit Lyonais, Nordbanke, and The Export-Import Bank of Japan. Thus, the banking system began taking shape and commercial credit slowly began to evolve. This laid the foundation of a banking infrastructure, essential for the development of entrepreneurial activity.

However, personal cheques for domestic accounts did not exist yet, and most entrepreneurs paid their employees in cash. With the US dollar worth over 10,000 dong, and 200 dong notes being common, cash transactions could literally involve truckloads.

© 1997 by Leo Paul Dana

Effective Handling of Cash

Meanwhile, foreign banks expressed their concerns: they could only repatriate 30% of their capital, and they were not given the three-year tax holiday granted to foreign entrepreneurs. Furthermore, there was a high tax structure for banks: 50% income tax as well as a turnover tax of 4 to 15%. In 1995, there were still only 50,000 bank accounts in Vietnam.

The Effect of *Doi-Moi*

Vietnam's model of economic transition is quite unique. It has achieved a harmony between government firms, still operating under a system of centralisation, and the small business sector, operating independently, while having access to state alternatives as specified by Resolution No. 16. Whereas transition from centralised planning to market economy in the Soviet bloc was very abrupt and economic reform in Yugoslavia very violent (Dana, 1994d), the *Doi-Moi* model of evolutionary change introduced a gradual and smooth transition in Vietnam. Small enterprises are thriving side by side with a state-controlled big business sector, the latter often looked upon as less efficient.

Most of the approximately 1,500 co-operatives now in existence are small to medium-sized businesses, many of which are being converted into companies. As well, there are countless micro-enterprises in the handicraft and agriculture sectors. The small business sector, including handicrafts as well as small industry, employs about two million people in Vietnam, and accounts for a significant part of industrial production and exports. Current exports include: bamboo products, bicycle tires and tubes, cotton yarn, glass products, handicrafts, processed forestry products, rubber gloves, and silk yarn. As well, crabs, frozen fish and shrimp are exported to Canada, Hong Kong and Singapore; furniture to Italy and Japan; garments to Australia, Canada, Japan and Taiwan; and hot water bottles to Hungary.

As a result of *Doi-Moi*, the small business sector in the Socialist Republic of Vietnam now includes co-operatives; family businesses; other private enterprises; and joint ventures between state and private interests. The first three operate free from state control; in the fourth case, government influence is limited to contractual agreement. By 1998, over 25% of retail sales took place in the free market.

Although the Socialist Republic of Vietnam has chosen to *retain* socialist ideals, to the ethnographer, Vietnam appears to be thriving more on free enterprise than on Marxist ideology. There is a constant buzz of mercantile energy.

Entrepreneurs optimise the use of their minimal resources, and make due despite a poor, but improving infrastructure. The spirit of entrepreneurship is in the air, even at the subsistence level. One villa advertises, "Telex Coffee Dansing Massage." Not far, a man sits by the roadside with a pump and fills tires, while another rents out the use of a scale. A coconut stand is never very far away, offering fresh coconut water.

In Ho Chi Minh City, one is overwhelmed by teams of children begging; or older ones, their arms overflowing with a variety of merchandise for sale, including pocket video games, T-shirts, cigarettes, fans, money from French Indo-China, and stamp collections. The young peddlers follow their prospective clients, for blocks on end, in an attempt to sell their goods.

Not far, one shed is a pancake restaurant when it is not being used as a bus depot. "Mr. Fix-It" earns his living by selling a wide variety of inventory, ranging from motorcycles and caviar to tiger-skins for $1,000 US. Further on, a woman sits on the sidewalk, feathering ducks. A man unloads fresh pork from a wooden container onto the street. Nearby, fish are being laid out in tidy rows; some of the fish are still flopping on the merciless, hot pavement.

© 1999 by Leo Paul Dana
Typical Street Scene in Ho Chi Minh City

At the market, items for sale include bananas, coconuts, dragon fruits, grapes, guavas, mint leaves, oranges, papayas, pineapples, and jeruk (green pomelos sweeter and larger than a grapefruit). Chicken, duck, fish, and pork are sold alive or dead, or in between. Also for sale is *xuxe*, a mixture of green peas, coconut and cane sugar wrapped in palm leaves fashioned into tiny boxes held together by bamboo toothpicks.

Apples are less common, except perhaps in Chinatown. There are one million ethnic-Chinese persons in Vietnam, of whom 57% are Cantonese. In Ho Chi Minh City, they make up 12% of the population. Yet, they control up to 50% of the local economy. Shoppers arrive in Chinatown by *cyclo* (foot-pedal version of a rickshaw resembling the trishaw as found in Singapore, but with passengers in front rather than beside the driver as in the case of the trishaw). Along the way, one encounters motorcycles bound for market, carrying bunches of ducks and chickens. Feathers seem to appear everywhere.

On every street corner, food is served, including rice soup, fish, duck, chicken, pork, vegetables and coconut paste. Most dishes are served in re-used plastic bowls, not necessarily washed between users.

Self-employed vendors also sell food to passengers on state-run trains. While some children run along the aisles fanning passengers, others sell sodas; the vendors open the bottles with their teeth.

Wherever the train stops in the morning, locals have washcloths for rent as well as buckets of water for passengers to refresh themselves. Through the windows of the train, merchants sell bread, coconut water, fruit, juice, pastries, and sodas.

Blind musicians come on board the train to sing or play a melody, while an assistant usually holds out a cap for donations. Simultaneously, one may buy a chicken breast with rice cooked in chicken fat, served on a palm leaf, and eaten with one's fingers. Other passengers prefer to crunch a raw, fertilised duck egg, just prior to hatching, feathers, bones and all, lightly salted. Still other passengers enjoy having a local cook board the train and flame a fish at their seat.

A glance out of the open window supplies passengers with constant stimulus. Abandoned Catholic churches line the railway tracks side by side with Buddhist temples still in use. Farmers waist-deep in rice fields, with water buffaloes as tractors, work their land in utter peacefulness while but a few kilometres away, remnants of a bloody war fill the landscape. Graves with crosses, graves with swastikas and graves with dragons adorning them dot the landscape, all with the hatred of war still hanging about them.

Some people live a few feet from the railroad tracks in shacks with no kitchen, toilet nor running water and subtle hands reach into the passenger compartment of the train. Others sling a hammock under the railway cars and alight where they choose, while still others enjoy a warm breeze sitting on top of the wagons as clandestine passengers.

In Hoi-an, the market is the life of the town. For sale at the market are *chuoi tieu*, a variety of bananas with an attractive colour and taste. A few minutes away, peaceful serenity reigns. Lining the waterfront are storefronts untouched for 200 years or more and buildings inscribed with Chinese characters dating back to the era prior to French rule.

Along the road to Hanoi, stalls display one-litre Coca-Cola bottles filled with kerosene or petrol for sale by proprietors of mini petrol pumps (with no pumps). Others sell fuel for cigarette lighters.

Every day, 50,000 peddlers transport their goods between Vietnam and China. Micro-enterprises involve exporters piggy-backing freight. Women, less expensive porters than are mules, many carry wicker baskets, each balanced at the end of a pole leaning across the shoulders. In the baskets are cats and dogs destined for Chinese dinner tables.

Although large state enterprises may be inefficient, people appear to have a strong work ethic. In contrast to China, where individuals dare speak up against their boss, the Vietnamese tend to be very disciplined, and with a mild temperament. As the state enterprises gradually lose their monopolies, a new middle class of *nouveau-riche* entrepreneurs is emerging.

Toward the Future

The small business sector will continue to be important to development of the Vietnamese economy in the future. Entrepreneurial firms may now be established rapidly, and they can produce quick returns on investment. In 1998, the average annual income in Vietnam was $340. Given the low level of wages, new ventures are likely to utilise labour-intensive technology, creating considerable employment. Small enterprises are flexible as to location, and may be situated in rural areas, thereby reducing development imbalances. This is line with government objectives.

There are nevertheless constraints, of concern to entrepreneurs. Tan and Lim (1993) reported that 80% of business people surveyed in Vietnam found bureaucracy and corruption to be major obstacles to enterprise. Venard explained:

> Vietnamese corruption arises from four factors: strict relations between the government and some private interests, decentralisation to regional governments which makes them more powerful and less controllable, under-payment of state employees, and vague laws governing commercial transaction (1998, p.87).

The government is being faced with the challenging task of dismantling bureaucratic structures no longer relevant to the economic model of *Doi-Moi*; simultaneously, there is a necessity for new institutions to be better prepared, in order to meet the needs of the future. A problem is that there is still an uncertain legal context of any investment. Although the foreign investment law guarantees against expropriation, a 1992 amendment gives the Vietnamese the "right" to acquire foreign shares of "important economic sectors." Another concern is the lack of established mechanisms for conflict and dispute resolution. Disputes have typically been referred to local arbitration panels, which have no enforcement powers.

Vietnamese entrepreneurs are faced with a variety of taxes: a complex tariff scale; local taxes; business turnover tax; and a personal income tax of up to 50%. Entrepreneurs often prefer to bribe an under-paid tax collector than to pay the taxes that they owe. Whereas Vietnamese entrepreneurs are heavily taxed, foreign direct investment is encouraged. Vietnamese entrepreneurs are therefore getting "foreign devil" companies set up in Hong Kong on their behalf. Profits are made in Hong Kong, resulting in less tax and less bureaucratic interference. A reduction in government intervention would allow entrepreneurs to concentrate more on business than on avoiding government regulation. Furthermore, given that Vietnam still has considerable import duties and that large-scale smuggling is known to occur, the entrepreneur who imports legally finds himself at a disadvantage. Appropriate government action should attempt to correct this.

Another issue of concern is dual pricing. A foreigner in Vietnam is required to pay up to ten times as much as is a Vietnamese citizen, for various services such as transportation. To the foreigner, this dual pricing system is not only perceived as discriminating and unfair, but also complicates decision-making. An enterprise needing to send a representative to a meeting might be influenced to send not necessarily the best individual, but the one whose ticket will cost 90% less.

Decades of socialist rule have put a damper on entrepreneurial know-how. Government promotion of the sector should include the training of entrepreneurs, provision of industrial estates and common facility services, including consultant services and labour relations services. Also beneficial would be access to financing for development, and industrial research. As well, small firms need assistance in procuring inputs, *i.e.*, raw materials as well as capital equipment.

Exports from the Socialist Republic of Vietnam were traditionally destined to former East Germany and other socialist countries where demand exceeded supply. Quality, marketing and advertising were not concerns. This needs to change in order to be competitive in today's changing marketplace. As entrepreneurs increase their share of exports, they will also need to learn about insurance, shipping, international banking, etc.

For years, South Korean entrepreneurs ordered textiles from Hanoi and shipped them home where South Korean labels were put on them. The Vietnamese products were then re-exported to the United States, under South Korean quota. Since the removal of the US embargo, Vietnamese exporters are permitted to play a greater role in the international arena. Yet, they lack experience and expertise. The government might assist by providing marketing information and assistance in exporting.

Taiwanese entrepreneurs are important investors in Vietnam. They bring technology, they create jobs, and allow Vietnam to benefit from their marketing skills and networks abroad, which contribute to exports. However, these people are concerned about what they perceive to be excessive government intervention in the economy. New legislation made it illegal to export more than $3000 US without lengthy bureaucratic requirements.

Until recently, considerable resources were being expended, in order to spread the socialist model throughout Vietnam. The economy of the south was integrated into the system of economic management that was developed in the north. Recognising deficiencies of its public policy, Vietnam introduced the *Doi-Moi* model, allowing entrepreneurship to gradually play an increasingly important role – without overthrowing the socialist establishment. Institutions and regulatory frameworks are slowly, but continuously, being adapted to the needs of the future.

Chapter 15

Toward the Future

Success depends on good timing, a proper environment and people in harmony.

-- Chinese proverb

This book has surveyed the evolution of public policy on entrepreneurship in different contexts. Although governments across Pacific Asia recognise the importance of entrepreneurship, the emphases of their respective promotion efforts differ greatly, reflecting national priorities, demographic factors and cultural values. Likewise, the entrepreneurship sector reflects historical and cultural factors, as well as public policy.

In Cambodia, the Khmer Rouge extinguished entrepreneurship, a sector which is slowly re-establishing itself, in an environment of uncertainty. In China, entrepreneurship is being promoted as a supplement to the socialist economy. In Indonesia, where the Chinese minority has been at the forefront of entrepreneurship, the state has been trying to promote entrepreneurship among the indigenous *pribumis*. In Japan, small-scale entrepreneurship is a complement to large corporations, and cultural values propagate inter-firm linkages. Credit policy in Korea resulted in *chaebols* squeezing many entrepreneurs out of business; government measures intervened to assist small-scale entrepreneurship. In Laos, cultural values discouraged entrepreneurship among Lao men, resulting in opportunities for women and foreigners.

In response to the domination of entrepreneurship in Malaysia, by ethnic-Chinese entrepreneurs, Malaysia adopted a policy of giving preferential treatment to indigenous *bumiputras*. The Chinese minority also dominates the entrepreneurship sector of the Philippines. In Singapore, multinationals saturated the domestic markets forcing the internationalisation of formerly local entrepreneurship. Taiwan has more entrepreneurs per capita than has

209

any of its neighbours. In Thailand, tolerance of Chinese entrepreneurship helped the sector to thrive. In Vietnam, entrepreneurship was introduced as a complement to socialism.

Different governments have designed a variety of programmes to promote the development of entrepreneurship. Much spending, however, is in vain, as entrepreneurship development programmes alone are insufficient. Programmes may be useful to those who know about them; often, those who could use them the most are unaware of their existence. Furthermore, policies which are not implemented fairly consequently fail to have the desired effect on society. In some economies, bribery, excessive taxation and regulation can inhibit entrepreneurship.

In each economy, the nature of entrepreneurship will evolve in time, but one should *not* expect entrepreneurship to converge across societies. There is no one formula for a "best" policy to promote entrepreneurship. Entrepreneurship is embedded in society, and the latter is affected by historical experience and cultural values.

Entrepreneurship must be understood in the context of national development. To be relevant, policies must be culturally sensitive.

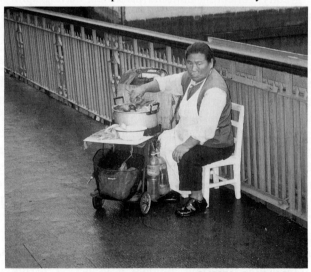

© 1999 by Leo Paul Dana

Waiting for the Future

Bibliography

Ahmed, Zafar U., Leo Paul Dana, Syed Aziz Anwar and Peter Beidyuk(1998), "The Environment for Entrepreneurship and International Business in the Ukraine," *Journal of International Business & Entrepreneurship* 6 (2), December 1998, pp.113-130.

Anyansi-Archibong, C. (1987), "The Role of Entrepreneurship in Economic Development," in Robert G. Wyckham, Lindsay N. Meredith and Gervase R. Bushe, eds., *The Spirit of Entrepreneurship*, Vancouver, British Columbia: Faculty of Business Administration, Simon Fraser University, pp.31-43.

Arendarski, A., T. Mroczkowski and J. Sood (1994), "A Study of the Redevelopment of Private Enterprise in Poland: Conditions and Policies for Country Growth," *Journal of Small Business Management* 32, pp.40-51.

Auster, Ellen and Howard E. Aldrich (1984), "Small Business Vulnerability, Ethnic Enclaves and Ethnic Enterprise, " in Robin Ward and Richard Jenkins, eds., *Ethnic Communities in Business: Strategies for Economic Survival,* Cambridge: Cambridge University Press, pp. 39-54.

Bandura, Albert (1982), "Self-Efficacy Mechanism in Human Agency," *American Psychologist* 36, pp. 122-147.

Bandura, Albert and N.E. Adams (1977), "Analysis of Self-Efficacy Theory of Behavioral Change," *Cognitive Theory and Review* 1, pp. 287-310.

Barth, Frederik (1967), "On the Study of Social Change," *American Anthropologist* 69 (6), December, pp. 661-669.

Barth, Frederik (1981), *Process and Form in Social Life,* London: Routledge & Kegan Paul.

Barth, Frederik, ed., (1963), *The Role of the Entrepreneur in Social Change in Northern Norway,* Bergen: Norwegian Universities' Press.

Befus, David R., Timothy S. Mecon, Debbie L. Mescon and George S. Vozikis (1988), "International Investment of Expatriate

Entrepreneurs: The Case of Honduras," *Journal of Small Business Management* 26 (3), July, pp.40-47.

Begley, Thomas M. and David P. Boyd (1987), "Psychological Characteristics Associated With Performance in Entrepreneurial Firms and Smaller Businesses," *Journal of Business Venturing* 2 (1), pp. 79-93.

Bijmolt, Tammo H.A. and Peter S. Zwart (1994), "The Impact of Internal Factors on the Export Success of Dutch Small and Medium-Sized Firms," *Journal of Small Business Management* 32 (2), April, pp. 69-83.

Boissevain, Jeremy and Hanneke Grotenbreg (1987), "Ethnic Enterprise in the Netherlands: The Surinamese of Amsterdam," in Robert Goffee and Richard Scase, eds., *Entrepreneurship in Europe: The Social Process*, Beckenham, Kent: Croom Helm, pp. 105-130.

Bonacich, Edna (1973), "A Theory of Middleman Minorities, " *American Sociological Review* 38 (5), October, pp. 583-594.

Brockhaus, Robert H., Sr. (1982), "The Psychology of the Entrepreneur," in Calvin A. Kent, Donald L. Sexton and Karl H. Vesper, eds., *Encyclopedia of Entrepreneurship*, Englewood Cliffs, New Jersey: Prentice Hall.

Brockhaus, Robert H., Sr. (1991), "Entrepreneurship, Education and Research Outside North America," *Entrepreneurship, Theory and Practice* 15 (3), Spring, pp. 77-84.

Bruton, Garry D. (1998), "Incubators and Small Business Support in Russia," *Journal of Small Business Management* 36 (1), January, pp.91-94.

Camilleri, Jean-Luc (1997), "The Impact of Devaluation on Small Enterprises in Burkina Faso," *Small Enterprise Development* 8 (4), December, pp. 27-33.

Carstairs, Robert T. and Lawrence S. Welch (1982), "Licensing and Internationalisation of Smaller Companies: Some Australian Evidence," *Management International Review* 22 (3), pp. 33-44.

Cavusgil, S. Tamer (1994), "Born Globals: A Quiet Revolution Among Australian Exporters," *Journal of International Marketing Research* 2 (3), editorial.

Chandra, Nayan and Rodney Tasker (1992), "The Gem Stampede," *Far Eastern Economic Review*, July 30, p.20.

Chau, Sandy S. (1995), "The Development of China's Private Entrepreneurship," *Journal of Enterprising Culture* 3 (3), pp.261-270.

Chen, Kuang-Jung (1997), "The Sari-Sari Store," *Journal of Small Business Management* 35 (4), October, pp.88-91.

Cherry, Robert (1990), "Middleman Minority Theories: Their Implications For Black-Jewish Relations, " *The Journal of Ethnic Studies* 17 (4), Winter, pp. 117-138.

Chinh, Truong (1977), "Firmly Grasp the Proletarian Dictatorship," *Vietnam* 225, September, p.1.

Communist Party of Vietnam (1991), *Seventh National Congress Documents*, Vietnam Foreign Languages Publishing House, Hanoi, Vietnam.

Dana, Leo Paul (1987a), "Entrepreneurship and Venture Creation – An International Comparison of Five Commonwealth Nations," *Frontiers of Entrepreneurship Research*, pp. 573-583.

Dana, Leo Paul (1987b), "Industrial Development Efforts in Malaysia and Singapore," *Journal of Small Business Management* 25 (3), July, pp. 74-76.

Dana, Leo Paul (1988), "More Small Business is Not the Answer for Peru," *Journal of Small Business Management* 26 (3), July, pp. 68-70.

Dana, Leo Paul (1990a), "Saint Martin/Sint Maarten: A Case Study of the Effects of Politics and Culture on Economic Development," *Journal of Small Business Management* 28 (4) October, pp. 91-98.

Dana, Leo Paul (1990b), "The Increasing Role of Entrepreneurship and the Small Business Sector in South Korea," *The Malaysian Journal of Small and Medium Enterprises*, 1 (1), December, pp. 42-47.

Dana, Leo Paul (1990c), "Towards an Integrated Needs-Related Policy on Entrepreneurship," *Canadian Journal of Administrative Sciences/Revue Canadienne des Sciences de l'Administration* 7 (3), June , pp. 25-33.

Dana, Leo Paul (1992a), "A Look At Small Business in Austria," *Journal of Small Business Management* 30 (4), October, pp.126-130.

Dana, Leo Paul (1992b), "Entrepreneurship, Innovation and Change in Developing Countries," *Entrepreneurship, Innovation and Change* 1 (2), June , pp. 231-242.

Dana, Leo Paul (1993a), "A Goods and Services Tax (GST) and the Small Business Sector: Some Canadian Reflections," *Australian Journal of Public Administration* 52 (4), December , pp. 457-464.

Dana, Leo Paul (1993b), "An Analysis of Strategic Interventionist Policy in Namibia," *Journal of Small Business Management* 31 (3), July, pp.90-95

Dana, Leo Paul (1993c), "The Trade Facilitation Model: Towards the Development of an Indigenous Small Business Sector in the Republic of Kenya," *Entrepreneurship, Innovation and Change* 2 (4), December, pp. 335-344.

Dana, Leo Paul (1993d), "Towards Internationalization of Entrepreneurship: Two Models in Eastern Africa," *Journal of International Business & Entrepreneurship* 2 (2), December , pp. 83-108.

Dana, Leo Paul (1994a), "A Marxist Mini-Dragon? Entrepreneurship in Today's Vietnam," *Journal of Small Business Management* 32 (2), April, pp. 95-102.

Dana, Leo Paul (1994b), *Enterprising in the Global Environment,* Delhi: World Association for Small & Medium Enterprises.

Dana, Leo Paul (1994c), "Entrepreneurship, Innovation and Change in Former East Germany: An Ethnographic Account," *Entrepreneurship, Innovation and Change* 3 (4), December, pp. 393-401.

Dana, Leo Paul (1994d), "The Impact of Culture on Entrepreneurship, Innovation and Change in the Balkans: The Yugopluralist Model," *Entrepreneurship, Innovation and Change* 3 (2), June, pp. 177-190.

Dana, Leo Paul (1994-5), "A Comparison of Policy on Entrepreneurship in Taiwan and South Korea," *Orientations: Journal of East Asian Studies* 1, pp. 83-94.

Dana, Leo Paul (1995a), "An Ethnographic Account of the Environment for Entrepreneurship in the Republic of Panama," *Entrepreneurship, Innovation and Change* 4 (4), December, pp. 347-358.

Dana, Leo Paul (1995b), "Entrepreneurship in the Basque Country: An Ethnographic Account," *Entrepreneurship, Innovation and Change* 4 (1), March , pp. 69-76.

Dana, Leo Paul (1995c), "Public Policy and Entrepreneurship in the Caribbean: Nine Styles of Policy," *Journal of Private Enterprise* 10 (2), Spring, pp. 119-141.

Dana, Leo Paul (1995d), "Small Business in a Non-Entrepreneurial Society: The Case of the Lao People's Democratic Republic (Laos)," *Journal of Small Business Management* 33 (3), July, pp. 95-102.

Dana, Leo Paul (1996a), "Albania in the Twilight Zone," *Journal of Small Business Management* 34 (1), January, pp.64-70.

Dana, Leo Paul (1996b), "Devaluation, Entrepreneurship and Change in Venezuela," *Entrepreneurship, Innovation, and Change* 5 (3), September, pp.245-251.

Dana, Leo Paul (1996c), "Self-Employment in the Canadian Sub-Arctic," *Canadian Journal of Administrative Sciences/Revue Canadienne des Sciences de l'Administration* 13 (1), March, pp. 65-77.

Dana, Leo Paul (1996d), "Small Business in Mozambique After the War," *Journal of Small Business Management* 34 (4), October, pp.67-71.

Dana, Leo Paul (1996e), "The Last Days of the Compañero Model in Cuba," *Entrepreneurship, Innovation, and Change* 5 (2), June, pp. 127-146.

Dana, Leo Paul (1997a), "A Contrast of Argentina and Uruguay," *Journal of Small Business Management* 35 (2), April, pp.99-104.

Dana, Leo Paul (1997b), "Change, Entrepreneurship, and Innovation in the Republic of Kazakhstan," *Entrepreneurship, Innovation, and Change* 6 (2), June, pp.167-174.

Dana, Leo Paul (1997c), "Stalemate in Moldova," *Entrepreneurship, Innovation, and Change* 6(3), September, pp. 269-277.

Dana, Leo Paul (1997d), "The Origins of Self-Employment," *Canadian Journal of Administrative Sciences/Revue Canadienne des Sciences de l'Administration* 14 (1), April, pp. 99-104.

Dana, Leo Paul (1997e), "Voluntarily Socialist Culture and Small Business in the Kingdom of Lesotho," *Journal of Small Business Management* 35 (4), October, pp. 83-87.

Dana, Leo Paul (1998a), "Small But Not Independent: SMEs in Japan," *Journal of Small Business Management* 36 (4), October, pp.73-76.

Dana, Leo Paul (1998b), "Waiting for Direction in the Former Yugoslav Republic of Macedonia," *Journal of Small Business Management* 36 (2), April, pp. 62-67.

Dana, Leo Paul (1999a), "Small Business as a Supplement in the People's Republic of China," *Journal of Small Business Management* 37 (3), July.

Dana, Leo Paul (1999b), "Small Business in Greece," *Journal of Small Business Management* 37 (1), January, pp. 90-92.

Dana, Leo Paul (1999c), "The Development of Entrepreneurship in Macao and Hong Kong: A Comparative Study," *Public Administration and Policy*, March.

Dandridge, T.C. and D.M. Flynn (1988), "Entrepreneurship: Environmental Forces Which Are Creating Opportunities in China," *International Small Business Journal* 6(3), pp. 34-41.

Desjardins, Thierry (1997), "Le Cambodge, royaume de la corruption," *Figaro,* January 1, p.4B.

Drabble, John H. (1973), *Rubber in Malaysia: 1876-1922*, Kuala Lumpur.

El-Namaki, M. (1988), "Encouraging Entrepreneurs in Developing Countries," *Long Range Planning* 21 (4), pp. 98-106.

Fan, Ying, N. Chen and David Kirby (1996), "Chinese Peasant Entrepreneurs: An Examination of Township and Village Enterprises in Rural China," *Journal of Small Business Management* 34 (4), October, pp.72-76.

Gadgil, Dhananjaya Ramchandra (1959), *Origins of the Modern Indian Business Class,* New York: Institute of Pacific Relations.

Gasse, Yvon (1982), "Elaborations on the Psychology of the Entrepreneur," in Calvin A. Kent, Donald L. Sexton and Karl H. Vesper (eds.) Encyclopedia of Entrepreneurship, Englewood Cliffs, New Jersey: Prentice Hall, pp. 57-66.

Geertz, Clifford (1963), *Peddlers and Princes: Social Development and Economic Change in Two Indonesian Towns*, Chicago, Illinois: University of Chicago Press.

Ghosh, B.C. and David B, Taylor (1995), "Marketing Practices," *Journal of Small Business and Entrepreneurship* 12 (3), July, pp. 40-49.

Gibb, Allan A. (1986-7), "Education for Enterprise," *Journal of Small Business and Entrepreneurship* 4 (3), Winter, pp. 42-48.

Grabinsky, Salo (1996), "Crisis in Mexico: Its Effects on Family Owned Businesses," *Journal of Enterprising Culture* 4 (3), September, pp.301-316.

Gray, Karin and Mark Allison (1997), "Microenterprise in a Post-Emergency Environment," *Small Enterprise Development* 8 (4), December, pp. 34-39.

Grosvenor, Gilbert M. (1971), A Graphic Look at the Lands and Peoples of Southeast Asia," *National Geographic* 139 (3), March, p.295.

Haley, George T. and Usha C.V. Haley (1998), "Boxing With Shadows," *Journal of Organisational Change Management* 11 (4).

Haley, George T., Chin Tiong Tan and Usha C.V. Haley (1998), *New Asian Entrepreneurs*, Oxford: Butterworth-Heinemann.

Halloran, J.V. (1991), *Why Entrepreneurs Fail,* New York: Liberty Hall.

Hazlehurst, Leighton W. (1966), *Entrepreneurship and the Merchant Castes in a Punjabi City*, Durham, North Carolina: Duke University Commonwealth Studies Center.

Hisrich, Robert D. (1988), "The Entrepreneur in Northern Ireland," *Journal of Small Business Management* 26 (3), July, pp.32-39.

Hisrich, Robert D. and Guyula Fulop (1995), "Hungarian Entrepreneurs and Their Enterprises," *Journal of Small Business Management* 33 (3), July, pp.88-94.

Hisrich, Robert D. and Janos Vecsenyi (1990), "Entrepreneurship and the Hungarian Transformation," *Journal of Managerial Psychology 5* (5), pp.11-16.

Hisrich, Robert D. and Mikhail Gratchev (1993), "The Russian Entrepreneur," *Journal of Business Venturing* 8 (6), pp.487-497.

Holmes, S. (1988), "Small Business Research," *The Chartered Accountant in Australia* 58 (8), pp.50-53.

Holmquist, Carin and Elisabeth Sundin (1988), "Women as Entrepreneurs in Sweden – Conclusions From a Survey," *Frontiers of Entrepreneurship Research*, pp. 626-642.

Hornaday, John A. (1982), "Research About Living Entrepreneurs," in Calvin A. Kent, Donald L. Sexton and Karl H. Vesper, eds., *Encyclopedia of Entrepreneurship*, Englewood Cliffs, New Jersey: Prentice Hall.

Hull, David, John J. Bosley and Gerald G. Udell (1980), "Renewing the Hunt for the Heffalump: Identifying Potential Entrepreneurs by Personality Characteristics," *Journal of Small Business Management* 18 (1), January, pp. 11-18.

Ivy, Russell L. (1996), "Small Scale Entrepreneurs and Private Sector Development in the Slovak Republic," *Journal of Small Business Management* 34 (4), October, pp.77-83.

Jenkins, Richard (1984), "Ethnicity and the Rise of Capitalism in Ulster," in Robin Ward and Richard Jenkins, eds., *Ethnic Communities in Business: Strategies For Economic Survival,* Cambridge: Cambridge University Press, pp. 57-72.

Johannisón, Bengt (1987), "Towards a Theory of Local Entrepreneurship," in Robert G. Wyckham, Lindsay N. Meredith and Gervase R. Bushe, eds., *The Spirit of Entrepreneurship*, Vancouver, British Columbia: Faculty of Business Administration, Simon Fraser University, pp. 1-14.

Kahin, George M. (1952), *Nationalism and Revolution in Indonesia,* Ithaca: Cornell University Press.

Kinsey, Joanna (1987), "Marketing and the Small Manufacturing Firm in Scotland," *Journal of Small Business Management* 25 (2), April, pp.18-25.

Kinyanjui, M.N. (1993), "Finance Availability of Capital and New Firm Formation in Central Kenya," *Journal of East African Research and Development* 23, pp.63-87.

Lee, Choong Y. (1998), "Quality Management by Small Manufacturers in Korea: An Exploratory Study," *Journal of Small Business Management* 36 (4), pp. 73-76.

Lin, Carol Yeh-Yun (1998), "Success Factors of Small and Medium-Sized Enterprises in Taiwan," *Journal of Small Business Management* 36 (4), pp. 43-56.

Liuhto, Kari (1996), "The Transformation of the Enterprise Sector in Estonia," *Journal of Enterprising Culture* 4 (3), September, pp. 317-329.

Martin, James H. and Bruno Grbac (1998), "Small and Large Firms' Marketing Activities as a Response to Economic Privatization," *Journal of Small Business Management* 36 (1), January, pp.95-99.

Meredith, Geoffrey G. (1984), "Small Enterprise Policy and Programme Development: The Australian Case," *International Journal of Small Business,* 3, pp. 46-55.

Meredith, Geoffrey G. (1989), "Successful Small Agro-enterprises as Catalysts for Small Enterprise Development in the Pacific: a Fijian Case Study," *Entrepreneurship & Regional Development* 1, pp. 371-180.

Morita, Keiko and John C. Oliga (1991), "Collective Global Entrepreneurship," in John C. Oliga and T.B. Kim, eds., *Proceedings of the ENDEC World Conference on Entrepreneurship and Innovative Change,* Singapore: Nanyang Technological University, pp. 450-451.

Nehrt, Lee C. (1987), "Entrepreneurship Education in Bangladesh: A Beginning," *Journal of Small Business Management* 25(1), January, pp.76-78.

Neshamba, A. (1997), "A Transition of Enterprises from Informality to Formality," *Small Enterprise Development* 8 (4), December, pp. 48-53.

Noar, Jacob (1985), "Recent Small Business Reforms in Hungary," *Journal of Small Business Management* 23(1), January, pp. 65-72.

Ojuka-Onedo, A.E. (1996), "Interventionist Policy in Enterprise Development Using the Rural Poor in Agrarian Developing Countries," *Entrepreneurship, Innovation, and Change* 5 (3), September, pp. 263-265.

Pache, Gilles (1996), "The Small Producer in the French Food Distribution Channel," *Journal of Small Business Management* 34(2), April, pp. 84-88.

Parnwell, Mike and Sarah Turner (1998), "Sustaining the Unsustainable? City and Society in Indonesia," *Third World Planning Review* 20 (2), pp. 147-163.

Patel, V.G. (1987), *Entrepreneurship Development Programme in India and Its Relevance to Developing Countries*, Ahmedabad: Entrepreneurship Development Institute of India.

Quesada, Fernando and Alvaro Mello (1987), "Empirical Observations on the New Social Entrepreneurship in Brazil," *Frontiers of Entrepreneurship Research*, Babson College, pp. 588-589.

Raghunanda, M. (1995), "Entrepreneurial Survival Skills in the Midst of Economic Chaos," *Journal of Enterprising Culture* 3 (4), December, pp. 463-482.

Redding, Gordon (1990), *The Spirit of Chinese Capitalism*, Berlin: de Gruyter.

Rondinelli, D. (1991), "Developing Private Enterprise in the Czech and Slovak Federal Republic," *Columbia Journal of World Business* 26, pp.26-36.

Sacks, P.M. (1993), "Privatization in the Czech Republic," *Columbia Journal of World Business* 28, pp.188-194.

Sarder, Jahangir H., Dipak Ghosh and Peter Rosa (1997), "The Importance of Support Services To Small Firms in Bangladesh," *Journal of Small Business Management* 35 (2), April, pp.26-36.

Sharma, S.V.S. (1979), *Small Entrepreneurial Development in Some Asian Countries: A Comparative Study*, New Delhi: Light and Life.

Silcock, T.H. (1967), *Thailand: Social & Economic Studies in Development*, Durham, North Carolina: Duke.

Silva-Castan, Jaime R., Luis Prott and Servulo Anzola-Rojas (1997), "An Innovative Program in Entrepreneurship Development at a Mexican University," *Journal of Enterprising Culture* 5 (1), March, pp. 1-12.

Simon, Hermann (1992), "Lessons From Germany's Midsize Giants," *Harvard Business Review* 70 (2), pp. 115-123.

Simon, Hermann (1996), *Hidden Champions,* Boston: Harvard Business School Press.

Siu, Wai-Sum (1995), "Entrepreneurial Typology," *International Small Business Journal* 14 (1), pp.53-64.

Swierczek, Frederic William and Somkid Jatusripatak (1994), "Exploring Entrepreneurship Cultures in Southeast Asia," *Journal of Enterprising Culture* 2 (2), July, pp. 687-708.

Tambunan, Tulus (1992), "The Role of Small Firms in Indonesia," *Small Business Economics* 4 (1), March, pp.59-77.

Tan, C.L. and T. S. Lim (1993), *Vietnam: Business & Investment Opportunities*, Singapore: Cassia.

Van der Land, Henri and Peniel Uliwa (1997), "Applying Subsector Analysis in Tanzania," *Small Enterprise Development* 8 (4), December, pp. 18-26.

Venard, Bernard (1998), "Vietnam in Mutation: Will it Be the Next Tiger or a Future Jaguar?" *Asia Pacific Journal of Management* 15, pp.77-99.

Walsh, James and Philip Anderson (1995), "Owner-Manager Adoption/Innovation Preference and Employment Performance," *Journal of Small Business Management* 33(3), July, pp.1-8.

Ward, Robin (1987), "Ethnic Entrepreneurs in Britain and in Europe," in Robert Goffee and Richard Scase, eds., *Entrepreneurship in Europe: The Social Process*, Beckenham, Kent: Croom Helm, pp. 83-104.

Weaver, K. Mark, David Berkowitz and Les Davies (1998), "Increasing the Efficiency of National Export Promotion Programs," *Journal of Small Business Management* 36 (4), pp. 1-11.

Weber, Max (1904-5), "Die protestantische Ethik und der Geist des Kapitalismus," *Archiv fur Sozialwissenschaft und Sozialpolitik* (20-21); translated (1930) by Talcott Parsons, *The Protestant Ethic and the Spirit of Capitalism*, New York: George Allen & Unwin.

Webster, L. (1993), *The Emergence of Private Sector Manufacturing in Hungary: A Survey of Firms*, World Bank Technical Paper 229, Washington, DC: World Bank.

White, Peter T. (1982), "Kampuchea Wakens From a Nightmare," *National Geographic* 161 (5), May, pp. 590-623.

Williams, E. E. and Jing Li (1993), "Rural Entrepreneurship in the People's Republic of China," *Entrepreneurship, Innovation and Change* 2 (1), pp. 41-54.

Wimalatissa, W.A. (1996), "The Emerging Class of Businesswomen and Women-Owned Business Firms in Brunei Darussalem," *Journal of Enterprising Culture* 4 (3), September, pp.287-300.

Yeung, Henry Wai-Chung (1999), "The Internationalization of Ethnic Chinese Business Firms from Southeast Asia: Strategies, Processes and Competitive Advantage," *International Journal of Urban and Regional Research* 23 (1), pp. 103-127.

Zapalska, Alina M. (1997), "A Profile of Woman Entrepreneurs and Enterprises in Poland," *Journal of Small Business Management* 35 (4), October, pp.76-82.

Index